PRAISE FOR *The Christian Parenting Handbook*

"Insightful, Practical, Encouraging and, as always, focused on reaching a child's heart rather than merely changing behavior. An 'aha' book that provides real-life help—help for everyday situations. Parents will keep this Handbook handy!"

—KARL BASTIAN, THE KIDOLOGIST, FOUNDER
AND PRESIDENT OF KIDOLOGY.ORG

"A must read for all parents no matter what faith or stage of life. This book is chocked full of practical strategies you can implement today! Having four teenagers, our house can feel quite chaotic. We are starting with the golden nuggets in chapter 15 right away."

—ERIC AND JENNIFER GARCIA, ASSOCIATION OF
MARRIAGE & FAMILY MINISTRIES

"Just as Wisdom offers inestimable rewards to those who find it (Proverbs 2:1–6 and 3:13–18), each chapter of this book provides a treasure chest of riches as the authors unpack God's wisdom. First, Scott and Joanne explain *why* families benefit when they implement biblical principles. They also introduce fifty principles that tell parents *what* to do. Finally, they suggest intensely practical ways *how* dads and moms can implement each one. Readers will mine nuggets of silver and gold on every page. I did!"

—MARK STEINER, PRESIDENT, DISCIPLELAND.COM

"The mission of parenting can be confusing and overwhelming. As Christians, we are not just looking for our children to act properly—we want to see them love and honor God with all their hearts! But what do we do, day in and day out, to shape the hearts of our children? The Bible has the answers! Whether you have toddlers or teens, the Bible-driven principles in this book have the power to change your family, for generations to come!"

—DR. ROB RIENOW, FOUNDER OF VISIONARY FAMILY
MINISTRIES (WWW.VISIONARYFAM.COM)

"As with anything Turansky and Miller write, this book is, as it claims to be, solidly biblical and thoughtfully practical. The truths they teach will convict, challenge, and inspire you to be the parent God created you to be. You will see yourself and your children in the pages of this book. Pay attention, and glean from the authors' collective experience and insight. You will come away with strategies that are effective, creative, realistic, and proven."

—JON SANNÉ, LEAD PASTOR, CALVARY CHAPEL OLYMPIA

"*The Christian Parenting Handbook* is another wonderful resource from Scott Turanksy and JoAnne Miller. As is customary, these two authors provide first a biblical approach to parenting. The format of this book provides parents with short, easy-to-read thoughts on key parenting strategies. It brings the type of practical advice I have come to expect from the founders of the National Center for Biblical Parenting."

—KENNETH PRIEST, TEAM LEADER, LEADERSHIP MINISTRIES,
SOUTHERN BAPTISTS OF TEXAS CONVENTION

"An artfully concise and biblically deep perspective for parents that dives into matters of the heart facing every child . . . highly recommend!"

—MICHAEL CHANLEY, EXECUTIVE DIRECTOR, INTERNATIONAL
NETWORK OF CHILDREN'S MINISTRY

"*The Christian Parenting Handbook* applies to all types of families including two parent, single parent, blended families, and grandparents parenting again. It is simple and easy to read yet so powerful in content. The techniques and ideas are broken down into short chapters, which makes it easy to pick up the book and find just what you need at the exact moment you need it. I will definitely be recommending this book to all the single parent families I work with and to children's ministers who call looking for parenting books."

—LINDA RANSON JACOBS, DC4K CREATOR AND AMBASSADOR
(WWW.DC4K.ORG), SINGLE PARENT EXPERT

"*The Christian Parenting Handbook* is undoubtedly a 'game changer' for most parents. Parents learn a biblical approach that aims at shaping the heart of their child rather than only outward actions. This is a handbook . . . practical and thorough . . . that will be used throughout the years of parenting!"

—DR. ROGER THEIMER, CHILDREN'S PASTOR AND
COAUTHOR OF *Faith Legacy Series*

"As a dad to four kids and someone who works with thousands of teenagers every year, I can tell you that Scott's and Joanne's approach to parenting really works. It is biblically rooted and designed to create long-term change, and it does. It has helped create peace in our own home. It's helped my wife and me minister to single moms with troubled kids. In fact, the honor-based approach to discipline is the basis of the student life component in our Summit programs and it has led to significant life change in many young adults. *The Christian Parenting Handbook* takes the best advice from the National Center for Biblical Parenting and puts it into solutions you can access inside of five minutes. Many moms and dads are discouraged and ready to give up; *The Christian Parenting Handbook* brings peace and harmony within reach, helping parents prepare great kids for a world desperate for honest, responsible young people."

—JEFF MYERS, PH.D., PRESIDENT, SUMMIT MINISTRIES

The Christian
Parenting Handbook

THE CHRISTIAN PARENTING HANDBOOK

50 HEART-BASED STRATEGIES FOR ALL THE STAGES OF YOUR CHILD'S LIFE

DR. SCOTT TURANSKY AND
JOANNE MILLER, RN, BSN

THOMAS NELSON
Since 1798

NASHVILLE DALLAS MEXICO CITY RIO DE JANEIRO

Published in Nashville, Tennessee, by Thomas Nelson. Thomas Nelson is a registered trademark of Thomas Nelson, Inc.

Thomas Nelson, Inc., titles may be purchased in bulk for educational, business, fund-raising, or sales promotional use. For information, please e-mail SpecialMarkets@ThomasNelson.com.

Unless otherwise indicated, Scripture quotations are taken from the HOLY BIBLE, NEW INTERNATIONAL VERSION®. Copyright © 1973, 1978, 1984 International Bible Society. Used by permission of Zondervan. All rights reserved.

Library of Congress Cataloging-in-Publication Data

Turansky, Scott, 1957-
  The Christian parenting handbook : 50 heart-based strategies for all the stages of your child's life / Dr. Scott Turansky and Joanne Miller, RN, BSN.
      pages cm
  Includes index.
  ISBN 978-1-4002-0519-6
  1. Child rearing--Religious aspects--Christianity. I. Miller, Joanne, 1960- II. Title.
  BV4529.T86 2013
  248.8'45--dc23
                           2012039114

Printed in the United States of America

13 14 15 16 17 RRD 6 5 4 3 2 1

To all the families in the United States and around the world who share a commitment to biblical parenting and have inspired us onward to develop practical, biblical parenting solutions.

CONTENTS

Introduction

Developing Your Own Biblical Philosophy of Parenting

You're holding a book of ideas. As parents, we need all the ideas we can find. Each child is unique, and the same tools don't work with every one. Furthermore, parenting ideas that had an impact last year may need some tweaking, because your child continues to develop and change. The suggestions in this book will help you be a better parent.

But you need more than ideas. In the parenting field, ideas are a dime a dozen. Everyone has an opinion of what's best when it comes to parenting. You probably have more ideas now than you can use. What you want to know is *how*. I'm sure you'd take a cup of implementation over a bucket of ideas any day. Ideas are easy. Implementation is hard, because that's where things get complicated. Every child is unique, and every family has its own set of dynamics. Parents are eager to know how to take ideas and put them into practice. We're going to help you with that.

But we're going to do even more than help you apply the changes. Each chapter in this book can contribute to your biblical philosophy of parenting. A philosophy is a way of thinking, a framework of ideas and theories. Our goal is to help you develop a biblical structure from which you'll be able to pick and choose from the advice and suggestions you'll receive in order to determine the best strategy for your home. By weaving together God's Word with practical applications, you'll begin to develop patterns that will make a tremendous difference in your life and the lives of your children.

Paul warned in Colossians 2:8, "See to it that no one takes you captive through hollow and deceptive philosophy, which depends on human tradition and the basic principles of this world rather than on Christ." That warning is important for parents, because our world is full of ideas, and many of them are unhelpful, resting on tradition instead of godliness. Instead, you can develop a parenting philosophy that's based on a solid theology of God and his plan for life.

Some elements of a biblical philosophy of parenting will be the same for every parent. Relying on God's Word as the authority, passing faith from parents to children, and teaching kids to live lives that follow Christ are important in every home. But many elements of a biblical philosophy of parenting will differ from parent to parent. Some will emphasize a more relational approach, where others are more firm. Some children need more structure than others to move them forward.

The formation of a unique, yet biblical approach to parenting provides parents with a way to think and act that's best for their family situation. The ideas represented in the chapters of this book will guide your thinking. You may choose to emphasize some more than others. Let the Holy Spirit guide you to develop your own unique approach. The common factor is reliance on God's Word for the development of your own philosophy of parenting.

Furthermore, you'll make adjustments along the way as you grow in Christ. In fact, before you get too far into this book, we suggest you create a quick action list, a reminder of what you want to *do* as you read through the chapters. Alongside your to-do list, though, we hope you'll create a *think* list, identifying key principles and concepts you'll use to guide your thinking over time. Each item on these lists represents a piece of your strategy, a biblical way of thinking about parenting and working with children. Together they'll help you formulate your own biblical philosophy of parenting. In essence, you'll develop a mission statement and a vision for your home and for each of your kids.

As you consider the principles in this book, you'll find yourself carving out a parenting style. You'll take your personality and allow it to be molded by a biblical framework and a grace-based, heart-based approach to parenting. In the end you'll find yourself growing faster than you had imagined in your ability to parent effectively.

Bear in mind that a heart-based approach to parenting involves strategic thinking, planning, *and* implementation. An idea is only an idea until it takes wings and flies into your home. It's not enough to have a good idea. You'll want to plan for its implementation as well. That's why many of the chapters that follow contain specific words you may use in your family. Our desire is to help you transfer good ideas into practical application that shape the way your family relates. As you formulate your own biblical parenting philosophy, please keep these principles in mind:

1. Begin with prayer, and ask your heavenly Father for wisdom, grace, patience, and perseverance. Praise God for progress and glimpses of maturity you see in your child.

2. Build on a biblical foundation. First and foremost, the Bible is the authority. It's amazing how many passages in Scripture apply to the family. Look at the Bible as God's training guide for life, and you'll discover many, many biblical truths that will impact your parenting. Every chapter in this book contains scripture to guide your thinking and mold your ideas.

3. Think long term. Maintain perspective by moving from the small picture to the big picture. Daily interactions are pieces of something much bigger. Misbehavior happens in patterns that reveal issues of the heart. Correcting any one instance can fit into a greater strategy to move kids toward maturity.

4. Remember what's most important. Focus on those things, and leave the rest for another time. To be most strategic in your approach, avoid "reactive parenting."

5. Watch for variations on a theme. It's not just about the moment. It's about life. Many times the challenges you face now fit into the bigger picture of the change that's needed.

6. Focus on the heart. Develop parenting plans that help children overcome internal roadblocks for the long term, not just current behavior problems.

More than anything else, we want this book to challenge you to think biblically, assess your situation, make adjustments in your parenting, and help your children move forward. We've compiled a list of fifty parenting principles that we believe to be the best we've seen over the years. We've worked with thousands of families and taught hundreds of parenting seminars. We've initiated many Bible studies and research projects. We've received tens of thousands of feedback forms. Out of it all, we've found fifty strategies that can make a significant difference.

With the information in this book, we believe you'll be able to develop a personal framework for parenting success. With strategic thinking and planning, you'll face daily challenges with more perspective, greater motivation, and confidence that you're moving in the right direction. Remember that God is the one who changes hearts, both yours and your child's, so read this book prayerfully, allowing God to speak to you about your relationship with him and what he wants for you and your family.

It's our prayer that you will find hope and wisdom in the following pages. Parenting is a journey requiring all the wisdom you can get, but having a biblical parenting philosophy in place will help you navigate through the challenges with greater ease and more confidence in God's grace at work in your life.

Parents often feel discouraged because they can't be consistent. They feel like failures. It's time to rethink some of the underlying assumptions proposed in many parenting approaches. In fact, the reality is that . . .

Consistency Is Overrated

"MY BIGGEST PROBLEM IS THAT I FEEL GUILTY WHEN I can't be consistent. Every parenting book I've read talks about the importance of consistency, but I'm running from here to there, getting things done, and my husband parents differently than I do. I feel like I'm failing because I can't be as consistent as I would like to be." Charlotte has three children, ages eleven, seven, and four. For the most part, she's doing quite well, but she's plagued with an overarching sense of guilt when things go wrong. The voice inside tells her the problems in her kids would go away if she were more consistent, but is that really the answer?

We've all heard that consistency is the key to good parenting. But many parents believe it's more important than it really is. If you're doing simple behavior modification, then consistency is essential. Giving the reward or punishment every time you see the behavior will reinforce change.

Behavior modification as a science began in the early 1900s. Ivan Pavlov made some exciting discoveries as he worked with dogs. If he consistently rang a bell just before he fed the dogs, he could eventually get the dogs to salivate by simply ringing the bell. This discovery of how to motivate a dog was picked up by John B. Watson in the 1920s, and he began to apply behavior modification to people. In fact, it wasn't long before behavior modification became a primary way to help people stop smoking, lose weight, and deal with a host of other behavioral issues.

In time, behavior modification influenced the classroom as well, and teachers used it to help children learn. By the 1950s behavior modification had also become the primary tool for parenting. Giving rewards and punishment to children worked quite well to modify their behavior. And one of the things parents and teachers all learned was that the key to behavior modification is consistency. The more consistent you are, the faster you'll see change. The problem is that behavior modification embraces humanistic thinking, the belief that people are just a higher form of animal. The Bible teaches something very different.

God created people different from animals. He gave each person a spiritual "heart," and that heart affects the learning process. The heart contains things such as emotions, desires, convictions, and passions. In short, the heart is a wrestling place where decisions are made. A child's tendencies come from the heart. When a child lies to get out of trouble, that's a heart issue. If a brother reacts with anger each time his sister is annoying, that's a heart issue too. Simply focusing on behavior may provide some quick change, but lasting change takes place in the heart. We're not saying behavior modification is wrong. We're just suggesting that it's incomplete and, in the end, lacks the depth for long-term and lasting change.

Parents who simply use behavior modification often end up with kids who look good on the outside while having significant problems on the inside. Consistency can teach kids to appear good, clean, and nice, but to help them change their hearts, other parenting skills must be added to the picture. Because you believe that God has created your child with a heart, you have access to an additional barrel of parenting strategies.

Rhonda, like Charlotte, found this principle particularly helpful. "I used to feel guilty all the time because I can't be consistent. I have four kids and a house to run. Invariably I'd have to sacrifice consistency in an area with one or more of my kids to accomplish my other tasks. When I realized that there's more to parenting than just being consistent, it freed me up to work on bigger goals with my kids. The consistency trap produced a lot of guilt in me. Now I realize that there's much more to parenting, and I feel freed up to use other tools as well. I'm continually asking questions about my children's hearts, and I'm learning a lot about how to mold and influence them to go in the right direction. I'm seeing more change in my kids with this new approach."

If you're training dogs to salivate, then consistency is essential. But you're trying to raise children. You don't want children to do the right thing just so they can get a reward. If you do, then kids learn to ask, "What's in it for me? What am I going to *get* if I do what you say?" Instead, you want children to change their hearts. You want them to ask, "What's the right thing to do here?" That shift in thinking is "heart work."

Developing a strong, biblical parenting philosophy requires you to embrace a more comprehensive approach that focuses on the heart. Looking beyond behavior modification calls for different parenting tools. When you focus on the heart, another quality becomes even more important than consistency: creativity.

The heart is where children hold their beliefs. It's where they develop operating principles about life. Kids learn through experience, stories, activity, and modeling. Sometimes children develop resistance in their hearts to a consistent approach. The same lecture from Mom or Dad over and over again builds up immunity through patterns of arguing, bad attitudes, and manipulation. Furthermore, when parents simply use behavior modification, kids tend to want bigger and bigger rewards for compliance.

Creativity has the ability to move around children's resistance and allows a truth to explode with meaning inside the heart. The best teachers are those who use creative teaching methods to communicate their point. Ed is mean to his sister. His father, Dave, is trying to help his son develop kindness. Sometimes he uses a consequence to correct Ed. Other times he requires an apology or has his son practice doing the right thing, requiring three acts of kindness before Ed can go. Dave is also having his son memorize scripture, and they've had several conversations about cruelty in the adult world. Dave is helping his son develop compassion for people, and they recently attended a Special Olympics event to gain a greater sense of empathy for others who are different. Dave will be successful with his son. It'll take time, but his commitment to creativity will help Ed develop a better response toward his sister and eventually to others in life.

Please don't misunderstand us. Consistency is important, especially when kids are young. But if you think more broadly about parenting and embrace creativity and strategy in your training, you'll be more effective at molding the hearts of your kids at any age. Your primary task as parent is to teach your kids, and a little work in the creativity department can make all the difference.

Deuteronomy 11:18–20 not only tells parents to train their kids but it tells them how to do it. Notice the creativity designed by God. "Fix these words of mine in your hearts and minds; tie them as symbols on your hands and bind them on your foreheads. Teach them to your children, talking about them when you sit at home and when you walk along the road, when you lie down and when you get up. Write them on the doorframes of your houses and on your gates." If you take that verse apart, you'll start thinking about your own home and your own kids and creative ways to teach them.

Even in Old Testament times, God knew that kids learn best through life experiences. Add creativity to your parenting goals, and you'll enhance your training tenfold. When consistency is unreasonable, don't let a lack of it produce guilt. There are other principles that are more important. Embrace a heart-based approach to parenting and you'll see lasting change in your children.

When you feel as though you're working on the same things over and over again and your kids aren't changing, it's important to remember the need to . . .

BUILD INTERNAL MOTIVATION

"I WISH MY KIDS WOULD DO THINGS WITHOUT ME having to prod them along every step of the way. I feel like I'm a cross between a drill sergeant and an inspector. We do the same things every day. Why can't my kids do it on their own?" That's a great question and a common feeling among parents. The goal is to help children manage themselves, but will that happen before they're adults? One mom said, "I'm afraid my kids will grow up and have to move straight into assisted living. They can't seem to do anything on their own."

Developing internal motivation in children is one of the fast tracks to help them toward maturity and being responsible. Unfortunately, too many parents use external motivators to get their kids to move forward. "If you get your homework done, you can go out and play." "If you clean your room, you can watch a video." This approach basically says, "If you do what I say, I'll give you what you want." Unfortunately, children trained this way often develop a mentality that focuses on external motivation instead of developing the internal motivations they'll need to be responsible and mature.

A continual reliance on external motivators takes advantage of a child's selfishness and exchanges a little gratification for a desired behavior. Children raised on heavy doses of external motivation develop attitudes of entitlement, asking, "What's in it for me?"

God is concerned with more than externals. He's interested in the

5

heart. The heart contains motivations, emotions, convictions, and values. A heart-based approach to parenting looks deeper. When parents focus on the heart, kids learn to ask, "What's the right thing to do?"

External motivation isn't wrong; it's just incomplete. When parents use a heart-based approach to parenting, longer-lasting change takes place. Parents still require children to finish their homework and clean up their rooms, but the way they approach the task of parenting is different.

Instead of just getting things done, parents have their eyes on other, heart-related issues. They're looking long term and often focusing on character. It's interesting to see that many of the misbehaviors that a child presents can be boiled down to a few character weaknesses. The job of parenting becomes more focused as parents are able to target specific heart qualities and require changes that adjust the patterns their children have developed.

Many children aren't quite ready to change on a heart level, so parents must be strategic. Sometimes that means more relationship to soften the heart, and other times it requires creating a "mini crisis" to show kids that the way they're living just isn't going to work.

A heart-based approach to parenting often shares values and reasons behind rules. It requires more discussions with kids, helping them understand that their hearts are resistant and that they need to develop cooperation. A heart-based approach is firm but also relational. It's a different mind-set for some parents and looks at the interaction of family life differently. Instead of simply getting the room cleaned and the dishes put away, parents are more interested in developing character, values, and convictions.

As you consider your kids, remember the words God said to Samuel when Samuel thought Eliab should be the next king: "Man looks at the outward appearance, but the LORD looks at the heart" (1 Samuel 16:7). That was a paradigm shift for Samuel and one that many parents need as well.

Unfortunately, you can't force children to change their hearts.

But you can do a lot to motivate them in the right direction. We've identified several tools that, when used properly, address the heart. Many of these are shared in the chapters of this book. Here are a few suggestions to get you started in reaching your child's heart.

Use sorrow instead of anger in the discipline process. Ann illustrated this well. She went out her front door to find that her eleven-year-old son had dropped his bike too close to the flowerbed, damaging some of her flowers. Her first reaction was anger, and she started imagining what consequence she'd give him. After taking a few deep breaths, Ann decided on a different approach. She calmed herself, went into the house, found her son, and with a flower in her hand, she said, "I'm so sad. I really liked this flower, but your bike landed on it, and now it's broken." She then turned and left the room.

A few moments later, her son came to her and said, "Mom, I'm sorry about the flowers. I know they're important to you. I'll be more careful with my bike next time." Mom was surprised. Usually her son would brace for her anger and immediately start defending himself. Ann was pleased that this time he was more responsive.

Parents who misuse this technique often lay a guilt trip on their children. The key is to be genuine. If you, as a parent, look past your anger for a moment, you'll see that you truly are sad about what your child has done because you know the long-term consequences of such behavior. Reflect it in a gentle way. Sorrow opens doors of relationship, whereas anger builds walls.

The Scriptures are also very powerful in the heart-change process because the Bible has an amazing quality: the ability to pierce through to the deepest areas of the heart. Hebrews 4:12 says, "For the word of God is living and active. Sharper than any double-edged sword, it penetrates even to dividing soul and spirit, joints and marrow; it judges the thoughts and attitudes of the heart." Don't use the Bible in a harsh way. Instead, reveal what the Bible has to say about being kind, respectful, or obedient. There's a lot of wisdom and conviction that come through the Scriptures.

Another way to help children change is to emphasize the heart, during times of correction. "I can see you're angry because I said no. I'd like you to take a break for a bit and settle your heart down and when you're ready, come back and we'll talk about it." A heart approach takes work, and a child may need a long time to settle down at first, but a change of heart is worth it in the end. Resolve the tension by having a positive conclusion or debriefing together. Address heart issues, not just behavior, and help children see things from a deeper perspective.

"What, then, is the place of rewards in child training?" you may ask. Should you reward your child for good behavior, or just expect it to be done? Rewards shouldn't be abandoned, but should instead be used to encourage the heart. Use them sparingly, because rewards often lose their effectiveness over time, requiring that you increase the reward to get the same result. A reward is best used as a motivation to jump-start a new plan, to get the ball rolling in the right direction.

The real issue, however, has to do with the difference between internal and external motivation. Internal motivation comes from the heart, the desire to do what's right. You want your son to be clean or neat as a result of an inner obligation of neatness. When children experience positive internal motivation for accomplishing something, it often makes them want to try even harder.

External motivation comes from the outside and includes things like praise, getting paid, having a treat, paying for a broken window, missing a privilege, or seeing disappointment in a parent's eyes. As you develop your own biblical parenting philosophy, look for ways to build internal motivation, not just rely on externals to get things done.

Here's the principle to keep in mind: external motivations are helpful if they build internal motivation. So even though you may give a star or check mark to a child, talk about character and heart change. "I'm giving you a star for cleaning your room, but the most important reward is in your heart. It feels good to have your room neat, doesn't it?" Or, for an older child, "I can tell you've been working on being responsible with your homework this month. I can see that you are even feeling better about getting assignments turned in on time. Here's the reward, but I'm sure the real reward is the satisfaction you feel inside that you're demonstrating responsibility."

After all, God uses rewards and punishment with us, but he's most interested in the inner motivations of doing the right thing and showing love to others for the right reasons. The Scriptures promise rewards for God's children, but the greatest reward we could ever receive from God is the internal satisfaction of pleasing him.

3

Parents sometimes move to consequences too quickly. Children need to change their hearts. Other tools are often more effective, so it's important to remember that . . .

CONSEQUENCES AREN'T THE ONLY ANSWER

"IF YOU DON'T CUT IT OUT, I'M GOING TO . . ."

"Do this or you'll lose the privilege of . . ."

"Get it done now, or I'm going to take away . . ."

If you find yourself typically going to consequences with these kinds of statements, then you may be relying on behavior modification more than is helpful.

Some problems that parents face with their kids are more difficult than others. Children who have annoying habits, who tease relentlessly, or who explode in anger have ingrained problems that can drive parents crazy. Out of frustration, some parents think these children need bigger and bigger consequences. They believe that the bigger the consequence, the faster the change. Then those same parents are disappointed because their kids don't seem to be any different after the correction.

Parenting is the toughest job in the world. It's important that you don't get discouraged. Perseverance pays off, and your determination to hang in there with firmness and love is often what's needed. As you consider consequences for changing behavior, however, there are a few things that will help you get further in your parenting strategies, and you'll want to embrace them in your biblical parenting philosophy.

Remember that the goal is a changed heart, not just punishment for doing wrong. A larger consequence may be needed to get the child's attention, but the real work takes place by helping children adjust the way they think and by training them to develop mature behavior. Often, many small corrections are more effective than one large consequence.

Many parents move to consequences too quickly. They see a child doing the wrong thing and they yell, "If you don't stop that, I'll . . ." and off they go into consequences to motivate change. Keep in mind that there is a finite number of consequences available to you as you train your child. If you overuse them, they wear out. Your parenting responsibility must go on for many more years, so look for other forms of training and motivation. A good biblical parenting philosophy emphasizes more than just consequences for correction.

For example, one way to help children move from negative patterns to positive ones is to practice doing the right thing. After a correction time, whenever possible, go back to the offense and practice doing it the right way. You might say, "I was standing about here, and you were right there, and you go ahead and ask me for a snack again. I'll say no, and you show me how to respond the right way based on what we've talked about."

It's easy to tell kids to stop doing the wrong thing or to assume they learn to do what's right based on the correction you've just given, but actually practicing the right response goes a long way in helping children make lasting changes. Something happens when a child replays the situation and does it the right way. It may look forced and seem as though you're just going through the motions, but sometimes that's just what's needed to help kids make the connection for the next times of life.

When kids have deeply rooted weaknesses, practicing the right thing can help change patterns. One mom had her five-year-old son stop three times a day to do kind things for others. At first he was resistant, but she made it fun, and he became creative with the project. A dad set up a plan with his fifteen-year-old daughter so that in exchange for trips to the mall, she'd look for ways to encourage Mom instead of fight with her. He was just trying to teach her that a family is a two-way street.

Sometimes parents assume that children know what the right thing is. After all, these moms and dads have been saying the same thing over and over again. But hearing it in their ears isn't the same as embracing it in their hearts. Life requires practice, and good practice builds healthy patterns.

Children need to practice doing what's right, not just receive correction for doing something wrong. This may seem obvious when you think about it, but it can be a challenge to get a plan working in family life. Parents are often motivated by their frustration and respond with correction only. Developing a proactive approach as well can make all the difference. It's amazing how a parent's attitude toward the child changes when both parent and child are working together in a positive direction.

Mature people feel an internal pain when they discover that they've made a mistake or done the wrong thing. This is normal and healthy. Your child may not experience that same inner sense yet. Consequences create a kind of pain for children. This pain can motivate right behavior and get them moving in the right direction. But don't just give the consequence without requiring some kind of positive action.

One example of this is the parent who decided to take away the privilege of riding a bike from her nine-year-old son. She said, "Son, I'm not just taking the bike away for a day. I'm taking the bike away until I see some progress in the way you're treating me when I call you in for dinner. We'll see how you do for a while, and if I see a good response, then you can have your bike back again." Mom turned the discipline around so that the child had to earn back the privilege. She wanted to see several positive change points before she allowed her son to ride his bike again.

Rarely is it helpful to set a time limit on a consequence. It's usually best to tie the return of the privilege to positive actions. In essence you're telling your child, "Show me that you can do the right thing, and then I'll allow you to have that privilege again."

When talking about the importance of obeying God's Word and not just listening to it, the Bible says, "Do not merely listen to the word, and so deceive yourselves. Do what it says. Anyone who listens to the word but does not do what it says is like a man who looks at his face in a mirror and, after looking at himself, goes away and immediately forgets what he looks like. But the man who looks intently into the perfect law that gives freedom, and continues to do this, not forgetting what he has heard, but doing it—he will be blessed in what he does" (James 1:22–25). This is great advice for being corrected by God's Word, but it's also helpful for parents when correcting their children. Practice doing the right thing to see that change is truly taking place.

Kids often need help to grow and change. Correction is just one of the tools God gave to help us learn in life. Require positive action to demonstrate change, and children will mature faster and learn more healthy responses.

4

When you feel overwhelmed because your child has so many weaknesses and problems, a good strategy is to pull back for a bit and . . .

IDENTIFY CHARACTER QUALITIES TO ADDRESS PROBLEMS

"SOMETIMES I GET OVERWHELMED BECAUSE MY CHILD has so many problems. I don't know where to start or what to focus on next. I hear advice that says, 'Choose your battles,' but I feel like I have so many battles to fight all at the same time. I don't want my home to be a war zone. I want things to be positive and to move forward, but I'm not sure what to do."

When you feel overwhelmed by your children's poor behavior, here's an exercise that will give you some direction. In fact, this activity is good for any parent looking for ways to help children grow, but it's especially helpful when you're confused and weighed down by a problem's complexity or deeply rooted nature. A strong biblical parenting philosophy requires that you do a bit of research and study of your child and the problem at hand so you know how to apply God's principles in strategic ways.

Take a piece of paper and make a list of your child's offenses or the problems you've seen in the last few days. This isn't a list to show to your child but is a working list so you can gain some perspective in your discipline. You're looking for examples of problems that need to be addressed. Look for behaviors, their causes, common arenas where the problem takes place, and others who were typically involved. In this step, you're simply gathering data and making observations, writing down the facts.

Next, group the problems by character qualities. That is, look for common threads in the offenses that may indicate a bigger heart issue. For example, one mom was discouraged with her son because he continually resisted chores, wasn't completing his work at school, and gave her a hard time when she asked for help around the house. She saw a common thread: her son didn't like to work hard and resisted work at every turn. She called it a "work ethic," but you could easily give it a character quality name, such as a lack of *perseverance* or *determination*.

Warren recognized that his son, Cory, had a problem with meanness. Cory was mean to his sister, made fun of people who were different from him, and liked to play tricks on people he didn't even know, just to get a laugh. When looking at the list of offenses, Warren was able to see that the real problem in his son's life was a lack of compassion. He began to look for ways to develop compassion in his son. Warren taught Cory to identify feelings in other people. They talked about hurt feelings and how humor can be offensive, and they went out of their way to help people in need. Over time, the behaviors decreased as Cory developed compassion in his life.

Grouping offenses around character qualities is freeing for many parents. First, it provides some perspective. Instead of working on fifty different negative behaviors, now you can focus on three or four positive character qualities. Furthermore, once you develop a strategy for character development, you begin to see many of the offenses in your child's life as opportunities for growth.

This approach also helps parents focus on what their kids need to be doing instead of simply focusing on the wrong behavior. Listen to your words of correction. Are they primarily focused on the problem, or on the solution? One mom caught herself in a trail of statements focused on the problem. "Cut it out." "Stop being annoying." "People aren't going to like you if you keep that up." Instead, she'd be more effective if she'd say, "Think about being sensitive." "Remember, stop and think first." "Look to see how the other person is feeling." By talking about the positive character quality you're developing in your child, you can be more positive and hopeful in your approach.

To keep character training practical, you may want to develop working definitions of the qualities you're focusing on. These aren't dictionary definitions, but are practical statements that give children hands-on ways to think about heart issues. Here are some examples to get you started, but the best definitions are those you develop that are targeted specifically to your child's needs.

Obedience is doing what someone says, right away, without being reminded.

Honor is treating people as special, doing more than what's expected, and having a good attitude.

Perseverance is hanging in there even after you feel like quitting.

Attentiveness is showing people you love them by looking at them when they speak.

Patience is waiting with a happy heart.

Self-discipline is putting off present rewards for future benefits.

Gratefulness is being thankful for the things I have instead of grumbling about the things I don't have.

One of the benefits of being a Christian is that the Holy Spirit comes into your life and produces fruit. Galatians 5:22–23 gives a list of character qualities that come from relying on God. "But the fruit of the Spirit is love, joy, peace, patience, kindness, goodness, faithfulness, gentleness and self-control." These aren't just qualities for your kids. Parents need these as well. In fact, the family is a great laboratory in which God helps each person develop the character qualities needed for life.

Now, when you see an offense in life, take time to identify the character quality your child needs to develop. You might say to a teenager, "I sense an ungrateful spirit in you, yet you seem to continually want me to sacrifice. I don't mind helping you, but I'm going to say no this time, and I'll watch and see if your gratefulness increases for the things I'm already doing for you."

With a preschooler you could say, "Remember, we're working on self-control. That means waiting sometimes without getting angry or upset." With an early elementary-age child, "When you come into the room, don't just start talking. Be sure to take time to see what's going on so you don't just interrupt other people. That's what we call *sensitivity*."

As your children grow and demonstrate godly character, be sure to affirm it. A little praise or even admiration for growth can go a long way. Admiration and gratefulness are two different things. Many parents are in the habit of thanking their kids for things, but many don't practice admiration. Thankfulness focuses on what a child does; admiration acknowledges who the person is or is becoming. For example, thank your son for taking out the garbage, but then go a step further by saying, "I really like that you did a thorough job. I admire that about you. You saw that extra bag of trash by the door and took it out too. Thoroughness is a great quality."

Admiration helps kids recognize character in themselves. A little work in this area can help children better understand how small tasks fit into the larger picture. Focusing on character is a great way to help both parents and kids maintain a healthy perspective on growth.

5

Parenting strategies tend to bring about change in kids. But sometimes kids have a hard time changing. In that case, you'll want to . . .

Transfer Responsibility for Change to the Child

PEDRO HAS A PROBLEM WITH MEANNESS. ABIGAIL leaves messes everywhere she goes. Connie tends to argue when she doesn't get her way. Many of the problems children have represent behavior patterns that need bigger heart-based solutions. When you see a negative behavior pattern, it may be time to work on it using a bigger plan.

When a child has a persistent weakness, he or she needs remedial work to raise the level of some kind of heart quality or aspect of character. Pedro is only five, but his parents can see that his meanness is a significant problem. He needs some work to build kindness into his heart so he can deal with his weakness. Abigail is ten, and her messiness is getting in the way of her success. She needs a plan that will raise her neatness factor to a level that matches her developmental stage. Connie is fifteen, and her tendency to argue has crossed the line of respect. She needs a plan to help her be successful in life.

If your son were five years old and couldn't walk, you'd get physical therapy to help him. If your daughter were ten and couldn't read, you'd get some tutoring to help her. The same is true when children have character weaknesses. They need remedial work to bring them up to a more functional level. Make sure your biblical parenting philosophy has a focus on character to address negative patterns you see in your child. Over time, focused attention in a particular area will do much more than a sporadic situational approach.

God calls that process *growth.* Second Peter 3:18 says, "Grow in the grace and knowledge of our Lord and Savior Jesus Christ." That growth sometimes just happens as children live life, but many times kids need concentrated effort to work on a particular area of weakness for a time.

If you find yourself nagging your child for the same thing over and over again, or yelling out of sheer exasperation because the same problem continually surfaces, it's definitely time for a different plan. One of the best ways to promote change is to transfer responsibility for that change to the child. Jesus often transferred the responsibility to others to help them grow. When the disciples told Jesus to send the crowd home so they could eat, he gave the problem back to them: "*You* give them something to eat." Then he allowed them to be part of the solution, feeding five thousand people (Mark 6:37; emphasis added).

Don't confuse this idea with natural consequences that children learn from life experiences on their own. That's a good discipline strategy and works when a child is motivated to change. For example, Abigail may be learning how to ride a skateboard, and her silliness results in a fall. Natural consequences avoid the "I told you so" mentality and allow Abigail to learn from life.

But Abigail isn't learning from life when it comes to her messiness. Dad and Mom have their own plan of pointing it out, disciplining her, and taking away her video game. Abigail doesn't like the plan, but she also doesn't seem to be changing. So they had a parent/child meeting and transferred responsibility for change to their daughter. They now start with affirmation and then challenge their daughter in a new way.

"Abigail, you're doing well in a number of areas. I like the way you're taking care of the cat, being responsible with your homework, and doing a better job at helping with dinner. I like the growth we're seeing in you. That's encouraging. There's one area, though, that we're seeing that's going to hinder your success in life if not addressed. It seems that you are tempted to leave messes behind instead of cleaning up. We believe it's important to help you deal with this problem.

"I have a 'Mom plan.' I'll take away your video game. But I'd like to help you develop a new strategy so I don't *have* to use the Mom plan. We're going to develop an Abigail plan. Here's a piece of paper, and on the top, I've written 'Abigail Plan,' but I can't write anything on this page by myself. This is your plan. I want you to think of some ideas to help you when you're tempted to leave a mess behind, so you can do the right thing instead.

"I'd like you to identify five things that you're going to do to help yourself deal with messiness. These are things that you're going to say to yourself and things that you're going to do differently. I can give you ideas, but I can't write anything on the paper, since this is your plan."

Abigail had a bit of trouble thinking of anything to write on the paper, so Mom said, "The other day I saw that you cleaned up the dining room table after you were finished with your school project. What happened there that helped you be successful?"

"I knew that you wouldn't be happy if I left that mess there."

"Okay, so one thing you could write on your paper is that when you leave an activity, you may want to think, *How might others feel about how I left it?* That's a good question to ask yourself. Why don't you write that down."

Mom continued to talk about the problem in ways that viewed it as Abigail's problem. Instead of focusing on her irritation, she described the messiness as a weakness that needed some work. Abigail put four things on her plan that would help her move forward. Over the next few days, as Mom continued to work with Abigail, she would ask her, "Which part of the plan would have helped you this time?" Abigail ended up adding three more items to her plan.

Now, instead of her typical approach to the messes, Mom looked for ways to hold Abigail accountable to her plan. The relationship changed between them. Mom now found herself acting more like a coach than like a police officer with her daughter. She began to see improvement. When she didn't, she would have to return to the Mom plan and remove a privilege or implement some other form of discipline. Over time, she began to see significant change in her daughter, and Abigail's plan seemed to be working.

Transferring responsibility to a child for a solution is strategic in a heart-based approach to parenting. Some children are resistant to seeing a problem as their own, and it takes work to transfer that responsibility, but requiring a child to take part in developing the plan for change helps that transfer take place.

The idea of transferring the problem to the child is a great way to help teenagers feel a sense of respect. When you come into your sixteen-year-old son's bedroom to get him to take out the trash, you might say, "This is Tuesday, and the trash needs to get down to the street. What's your plan?"

"I'll do it later."

"That's fine. I'd just like a time. Then I won't bother you about it because I know you have a plan."

"I'll do it before I go to bed."

"You need to get it done sometime before dinner. I'd like a time."

"Okay. Five o'clock."

"Great."

Now you can leave him alone until 5:00 p.m. and see if he does what he said he was going to do. If, on the other hand, he is just putting you off and waiting for you to remind him again at 5:00 p.m., then you have a responsibility problem. You may have to say, "Son, we have a problem. I want to give you an opportunity to discipline yourself so I don't have to discipline you. When you tell me you're going to do something, it's important to keep your word. If you can't do that, then we'll have to go to my plan; that is, to take out the trash on my schedule, not yours. I want to treat you with respect, but you have to be able to take responsibility yourself for things."

More discipline and consequences may be necessary at times, but the approach of transferring responsibility to a child is an essential ingredient to a solid biblical philosophy of parenting. One of the benefits is that it moves the parent more toward a coaching mentality with kids. Sometimes children need firmness to build character, but often, working as a coach with your child can accomplish more in the end. There's not just one good way to parent. The ability to approach a problem in multiple ways often pays off with more change than one single technique.

6

The business of family life is often about keeping kids on track and moving forward. But in the midst of all that work, don't forget . . .

THE RELATIONAL SIDE OF PARENTING

DO YOU EVER FEEL AS THOUGH THE ATMOSPHERE IN your home has turned negative because you have to do so much correcting? You know your children need correction, but at the same time you feel the discipline is taking its toll on the positive environment you want in your home. It may be time to do a relationship check to make sure your family life has a good balance between building close relationships and appropriate correction.

Children need firmness, direction, limit setting, instruction, and correction. But don't forget, they also need a lot of love, teaching, grace, affirmation, appreciation, and relationship. Of course, you know that, but it's good to be reminded every once in a while, especially when the business of family life gets intense.

Love can come in the form of affirmation, encouragement, support, or just spending time together. Connecting with a child's heart happens in different ways, but one sure way for your child to feel connected to you is when you show empathy.

Empathy is communicated by validating the pain or disappointment your child is experiencing. Then you can gently move into suggestion mode, if needed. For example, when the cat scratches your three-year-old son, who is playing rough, a lecture may not be the best approach. Instead, you might say something like, "Ouch! I'll bet that hurt. It looks like he doesn't like rough play, does he?"

Or when your eight-year-old daughter is hungry before dinner because she refused to eat lunch, you could say, "I'll bet you're hungry. That's a long time to go without food."

If you leave out the empathy and just move into firmness mode, children may react poorly. They may view your approach as condescending or cold and respond with anger or hostility. Empathy communicates love, while at the same time allowing the child to accept responsibility for the problem.

Empathy reveals understanding and care and validates the emotions a child is experiencing even though the actions that come out of those emotions may need correction. Demonstrating concern while your child learns from experience can be one of the best ways to develop closeness. It puts you on your child's team, facing the challenges life presents.

One dad said it this way: "I'm a problem solver. In fact, I show love to my kids by helping them solve their problems. Unfortunately, my teenage daughter sometimes doesn't want solutions from me. She's very capable of solving problems herself. When she shares a problem with me and I go into my solutions mode, she feels uncared for, just the opposite of what I want. I've learned that sometimes the best approach is for me to first empathize with her and imagine what she must be feeling. It's interesting that once I do that, she sometimes asks me for advice, and I can then help her solve her problem. The key for our relationship, though, has been my willingness to connect with her on an emotional level."

If you launch into solutions before a child is ready, you may find yourself getting frustrated at your child's lack of responsiveness to your advice. If you're wondering whether your child wants help or sympathy, you can simply ask; but going the empathy route is usually the safest. Then you can try to offer suggestions. "Would you like an idea?" you could ask, or "Would you like to hear how other people solve that problem?"

A listening ear communicates emotional connectedness. It says, "I'm interested in your world and how you think about things." Do you know your child's favorite activities, foods, and subjects in school? That's often a great way to start a conversation, because you're focusing on your child.

Relational connectedness is experienced in the heart. Acts 4:32 says that the early disciples were "one in heart and mind." Jonathan's armor-bearer expressed unity with his boss by saying, "Do all that you have in mind . . . I am with you heart and soul" (1 Samuel 14:7). Your enjoyment of your kids creates a connectedness that runs deep. With all the challenges of family life, close relationships help ease the tension. That's why 1 Peter 4:8 says, "Love covers over a multitude of sins."

When you come to the conclusion that changes need to take place in your child and that it's time to put your foot down because you just can't live this way anymore, think relationship first. Usually parents start imagining the consequences and how they're going to be more firm. Those are important components of your plan, but don't forget to add relationship. Children can only take as much pressure as the relationship allows.

Many times parents enjoy their children in ways that the parents prefer. They plan the activities and invite the kids to come along. Consider, instead, giving your child a gift of a half hour doing something he or she likes to do. I (Scott) remember one time when I did this with my children. Melissa chose to spend our time playing with dolls. I remember that being one of the longest half hours of my life as we dressed dolls and pretended all kinds of things together. I enjoyed being with my daughter, but playing with dolls certainly wasn't high on my list of enjoyable experiences.

In that activity, however, I realized that I often enjoy my kids my way. It just reminds me that I need to continually get to know my kids' unique qualities and try to understand their special likes and dislikes.

God does a lot of instructing, correcting, and limit-setting for us as his kids, but his primary desire is to have a personal relationship with us. All the other things flow from that. In Revelation 3:20, Jesus expressed his desire for relationship by saying, "I stand at the door and knock. If anyone hears my voice and opens the door, I will come in and eat with him, and he with me." Remember that relationship is foundational to all the other things that need to get done in family life.

7

Parents sometimes get discouraged. Kids can get discouraged too. Many times children need perspective that provides motivation to do what's right. Parents can help their children think beyond the present challenges when they . . .

ENVISION A POSITIVE FUTURE

TOM IS EIGHT YEARS OLD AND OBVIOUSLY DISCOUR-
aged. He has a problem managing his emotions and explodes with
anger a lot. That means he receives a lot of correction from his parents, teachers, and even from life itself. Dad and Mom are using
several strategies to help Tom gain control of his anger, but his discouragement is compounding the problem. Tom's parents realized
they needed to add a dimension to their strategy for Tom. In fact, it's
a strategy all our children need in order to maximize change in their
lives. It's a tool for bringing hope into the change process. Here's
what it looks like.

Most kids spend their time thinking about the present, what
they'll do today or tomorrow. When they look at the future, they may
have some wishes, but imagining themselves as successful is quite a
stretch for most. This is especially true of children who are a challenge
to parent. They usually experience a lot of correction, causing doubt
as to whether they'll ever be successful in life.

One element of a biblical parenting philosophy is to help children
envision a positive future. Take a few minutes and imagine what your
children will be like as adults. Some parents have immediate thoughts
of terror and doom, but instead, look at the good qualities your children have now, and imagine how those qualities will benefit them
later in life. Then share those observations with your children.

Envisioning a positive future looks beyond the day-to-day discipline and says, "I see qualities in you that are going to make you successful." It makes statements such as, "With that kind of thoughtfulness, you're going to make a great husband" or "Your thoroughness is going to make you a valuable employee someday." When parents learn to view their children this way, they look past the daily grind of parenting to what their children are becoming. "What is my child good at? What do I see now that will bring success as my child grows?"

Children believe what their parents say about them. If a parent tells a child he'll never amount to anything, the child is likely to incorporate that into his belief about himself, and it may end up becoming true. You can take that same principle and teach your children to see the growth in themselves and the specific ways God has blessed them.

Some children are magnets for correction. Every time you turn around, you're correcting them for one thing or another. Those kids often begin to develop a rather negative view of themselves. They have a hard time envisioning a positive future because the present is full of things they do wrong. Children tend to live in the present, and belief that change is possible can be elusive. They don't have enough life experience to help them see that things change and improve over time. They sometimes get caught in a dismal view of their lives, stuck perpetually in the present.

Spend time helping your kids see the growth they've already experienced and the benefits of the work they're currently doing to curb negative habits, develop self-control, and become more responsible. Interestingly enough, giving your children a positive vision for the future encourages them to live up to it now. The qualities you focus on end up being the ones they see in themselves and tend to develop.

Matt said it this way: "I feel like my son Robert has several weaknesses, and we're working on them, but he also has some strengths. He's sympathetic and sensitive to others' pain, for example. We had a fun conversation over dinner the other day. I told Robert that his sensitivity is rare and a good thing, and that it'll help him a lot when he gets older. He gave me that puzzled look, so I gave him some ideas about how sensitivity is a good adult quality. Maybe he'd want to help people who are hurt by working in a hospital or by becoming a counselor. Or the quality will just be helpful in making him a good husband and father someday. It was fun to watch the wheels turning in his head. He'd obviously not thought about that before and was encouraged."

Even when you correct your kids for their weaknesses, take time to explain why. It's not just because they've inconvenienced you or made you angry. It's because you see they're lacking a quality necessary for their future success. You don't want to overemphasize deficiencies in children so that they feel they don't measure up, but you do want to give them a vision for developing positive qualities for the future.

Each time you discipline your child, you're doing so because you want that child to grow up to be responsible and healthy. Instead of focusing on what your son or daughter did wrong, take time to emphasize the positive quality you're trying to develop. Kids may resist, and it may look as if they aren't listening to what you're saying, but don't get discouraged. You'll be surprised at how much they pick up from your correction and teaching.

Emphasizing a child's strengths, or even potential strengths, nurtures a child's heart. It's important to maintain a healthy balance in parenting between pointing out the negative and revealing the positive aspects of a child. It's true that a sin nature corrupts all human hearts and that the solution is a relationship with Jesus Christ. As children grow, they need to incorporate the Lord into more and more areas of their lives. Even if children don't love the Lord as you do, you can give them a vision for it by treating them as part of God's family. In this way you don't stop sharing about the need for repentance, but you also talk a lot about the benefits of knowing Jesus.

Envisioning a positive future gives your children hope and direction. It says, "You're going to make it. I believe in you." It's a way to honor your kids. When you help your children see a positive future, you're giving them a gift that will last a lifetime, a hopeful way of looking at themselves and their lives.

After all, God does this for us on a regular basis. Verses like Jeremiah 29:11 give us hope to live now to the fullest: "'For I know the plans I have for you,' declares the LORD, 'plans to prosper you and not to harm you, plans to give you hope and a future.'"

Humanism looks at the strength of personal potential only. Godliness relies on God's grace. As you continue to point out your child's strengths, be sure to talk about the Lord and his work in your child's life. You don't just want kids to believe they're good. You want them to believe they are recipients of God's grace. Envisioning a positive future provides you with an opportunity to give your children a snapshot of God's grace at work in their lives, both now and down the road as well.

8

Kids are in process and often need to develop new thinking patterns. Parents must always be ready to take advantage of opportunities when a child is most receptive to input. That's why parents must regularly . . .

Look for Heart Moments

When eight-year-old Jordan says to himself, "I'm no good. No one wants to be with me. I'll never get it right," he's repeating negative things in his heart. Rebecca feels good in her heart because she refused to join those who were disrespectful to the teacher. Michael's mom can see a heart problem because he scowls and complains whenever she asks him to do something. In each of these situations, the heart is at work.

Jordan, Rebecca, and Michael are all illustrating the fact that we say things to ourselves in our hearts. David wrote in Psalm 19:14, "May the words of my mouth and the meditation of my heart be pleasing in your sight, O Lord." What people meditate on is important, because those thoughts take place in the heart and eventually come out in actions.

The heart is where we wrestle with things. When experience, teaching, and values need to be integrated into life, it happens in the workshop of the heart. Information comes into our heads on a regular basis, but much of it just stays there. Only when it moves down to our hearts does it become part of our lives.

When parents use a heart-based approach, they take advantage of this wrestling inside a child. They encourage right thinking, contribute praise for growing character, and comment about the helpful and unhelpful internal dialogue as it makes its way out through behavior.

When the teachers of the law were struggling inside with the fact that Jesus forgave the paralytic in Matthew 9, he said, "Why do you entertain evil thoughts in your hearts?" (v. 4). When the two disciples on the road to Emmaus realized that their surprise guest was Jesus, they reflected on the experience by saying, "Were not our hearts burning within us while he talked with us on the road and opened the Scriptures to us?" (Luke 24:32). In both cases the heart was at work inside, wrestling with the information presented, trying to integrate it into life.

Look for ways to create heart moments in your child. Ralph was disrespectful to his dad, yelling and saying mean things when Dad refused to buy the latest computer game that Ralph's friends had. Dad decided to correct his son but wanted more than just lip service. He wanted to touch his heart. First Dad had Ralph sit in the hall and settle down. That took over an hour as Ralph continued to seethe and pout. When Ralph finally returned, Dad explained to Ralph that the temper tantrums were unacceptable and that he, as a dad, had a responsibility to discipline his son to try to help him. Therefore, Ralph would lose the privilege of the computer altogether for a while.

Of course, that news threw Ralph into another bout of ranting. Dad refused to join into the anger scene and sent his son back to the hall to settle down again. This time it took a half hour before Ralph calmed down and wanted to know when he'd get his computer privileges back. Dad calmly explained, "I've not set a time on it. I want to see some improvement in the way you handle correction and a no answer. Also, I'd like to see you come to me and ask if there's any way that you can help, and I'll give you some jobs. Over the next few days, if you can show me that you are trying to change the way you relate to me, and think about me and not just yourself, then we'll try going back to the computer."

Then Dad waited. Would his plan work, or would it need some adjustment? Dad knew what he was looking for. He wanted to see a sense of cooperation and self-control in his son. Over the next few days, he saw the heart moments he was looking for. Ralph volunteered to help and had a good attitude. Dad told Ralph no on a couple of occasions, and Ralph, though disappointed, was obviously trying to respond with self-control. Dad gave his son's computer privileges back, but only after they talked about the positive changes that were starting to occur. Ralph is still learning and growing, and complete change will likely take several years, but Dad corrected with an eye on the heart and felt that he made significant progress in that one incident.

Too many parents focus only on behavior, things like getting jobs done around the house and completing homework. Although those things are important, the real work of parenting is done in the heart. Be on the lookout for heart moments. They may surprise you at times. Be ready for them, because they don't come as often as you'd like.

Jesus frequently took advantage of heart moments. One day he told a rich young man, "If you want to enter life, obey the commandments." But then he went even further, telling the young man exactly what he needed to do to please God: give his riches to the poor (Matthew 19:17, 21). Jesus challenged him on a heart level. Here are just a few more examples of heart moments you may relate to.

Sarah made a nice card for her dad for Valentine's Day. It obviously took a lot of love and care to put it together. Dad realized that it was not just a card; it was a gift of his daughter's heart. He spent some extra time enjoying the card and his daughter, further encouraging her love and compassion.

Alberto made a comment about something he learned at church. Mom asked some more questions and discussed the issue with her son, realizing it was a heart moment. She talked further with Alberto, helping him develop the truth so it had an even greater impact on his thinking.

Kevin realized his daughter was hurt by a friend at school. Instead of telling her to just stop crying about it, he recognized that it was a heart moment and comforted his daughter. She obviously appreciated her dad's love and care, and just his presence with her for several min-utes helped her work through the issues in her heart.

Every morning when you get up, pray for your kids. Ask God to reveal opportunities for heart moments with them. You'll be amazed at the difference it makes in your family. Proverbs 20:5 reminds us that "the purposes of a man's heart are deep waters, but a man of understanding draws them out." A heart-based approach to parenting isn't easy, but it's where the significant work is done in a child's life.

9

Tension often increases in family life when parents don't adjust their parenting strategies to match the new stage of development in their child. Therefore, it's important for parents to . . .

MAKE PARENTING SHIFTS

PATRICIA IS EAGER TO BE THE BEST MOM SHE CAN BE, but she finds parenting a daunting task. Here's how she put it: "Just when I think I have it down, then something changes, and I have to make major adjustments. Parenting well feels like a moving target." Patricia is correct. Good parents are always learning and growing, but there's one strategy to keep in mind as your children grow and change. When a child moves into a new developmental stage, you must make a parenting shift to meet the new developmental needs and abilities.

Much research has been done on the developmental stages of childhood. Babies learn to sit up, then crawl, and finally walk. Kids have a greater ability to reason as they get older, and logic makes sense as they move further into preadolescence. A logical implication of these developmental changes is that parents will need to make parenting shifts along the way. Some of those changes are minor or subtle; others are more significant.

Parenting is a growing experience. You'll want your biblical parenting philosophy to allow flexibility to adapt to your child's changing needs. Unfortunately, some parents get ideas in their heads about what good parenting is, and then they lack the flexibility necessary to be effective. Although a strategy may work well at one stage, it may be necessary to modify or even abandon it at another.

For instance, when that tiny infant comes home from the hospital, the baby quickly becomes the focus of attention. The newborn sets the schedule for feedings and sleeping. Often both parents have to adapt their lives around one small child. However, as your baby begins to grow and develop, you change too. You no longer jump for every cry. You begin to set limits on a mobile child and determine a meal schedule for a toddler. Infancy requires that the parent give up an agenda and respond quickly to a baby's needs. As the child gets older, a parenting shift takes place, and the parent requires a child to wait more, fit into a schedule, and learn to consider the needs of others.

Some parents try to simplify their jobs by setting policies they think will last for years, apparently believing that one parenting approach fits all. One dad said about his one-month-old son, "I'm going to stop the teenage rebellion right here." He proceeded to set some pretty strict rules about feeding and sleep times, forcing his new infant into a schedule, to establish his authority. That's a sad misunderstanding of developmental needs and abilities.

Paul acknowledged a spiritual parenting shift in 1 Corinthians 3:1–2: "Brothers, I could not address you as spiritual but as worldly—mere infants in Christ. I gave you milk, not solid food, for you were not yet ready for it." Even spiritually, we go through shifts in our thinking and, as a result, can learn more about God's grace over time.

At each stage of development, parents must make modifications in their approach. A young baby must have physical and emotional needs met continually in order to develop a sense of security and to view the world as a safe place. As children grow to be toddlers or preschoolers, they need to develop two primary character qualities: responsiveness to authority, and self-control. Elementary-age children need opportunities to solve problems for themselves and a lot of teaching regarding responsibility, what it is and how it works. Teens need a completely different approach, carefully balancing firmness with extra dialogue as they develop their own value systems and decide who they're going to be as adults.

Considering your child's developmental level and making appropriate parenting shifts can make all the difference between a child who accepts your guidance and one who resists your leadership. Don't make the mistake of thinking that just because you allow your infant to eat on "demand," she'll be demanding when she grows up. On the contrary, infancy is a time to build trust and bonding, and that often comes with fast response to babies' needs. Several stages of growth and maturity will take place between now and adolescence, and you'll have plenty of opportunities to make adjustments that affect patterns in their lives.

Another example of failure to make the necessary shift is when the preschooler is running the house. If parents still treat a three-year-old as if he's a three-month-old, self-centeredness increases and hampers interpersonal relationships. It's usually not too long before parents realize the need to adjust and impose more limits. When parents are slow to make the needed parenting shifts at any age, children develop more dramatic symptoms to awaken parents to the need for change.

Often the signs of a need for a parenting shift are increased friction and frustration in family dynamics. If family life isn't working, a number of causes may need attention. Most of the time it means that parents will have to change the way they work with their kids. The old methods of relating don't work the same way anymore. In fact, they seem to cause problems instead. Sometimes the parenting shift is a result of developmental changes. Other times a different approach is needed because of a child's personality or a growing character weakness.

As your children grow, be ready to grow with them and make the necessary changes to influence them effectively. Even the best parents must make some changes in the way they parent as their children grow up. When children move into adolescence, you'll want to adjust many of the ways you relate. Although you may have been able to "control" young children, the key word for teenagers is *influence*. Firmness is still important, but more so now than ever, you're looking for ways to convince, persuade, and communicate the best way to live.

Change takes time, and your influence will produce the greatest results. Parenting is a complicated job with very few easy answers. The responsibility requires continual growth and flexibility to work with your child's changing needs. Furthermore, having multiple children requires that parents work on several levels all at the same time. Rarely does it work to treat all children the same, because each one needs something different.

To maximize your parenting, you must be a student. Your continued growth is essential. Studying God's Word will give you rich insights into your children, and reading parenting books and attending seminars will give you added tools to help your family. Study each one of your children to help develop a unique plan for that child. Be willing to make changes along the way and you'll have the most success.

10

When you get the sense that your parenting has lost focus and you're just reacting to problems, it's best to stop and realize that . . .

Parenting Is an Investment— Think Long Term

CAROL YELLS AT HER KIDS MUCH MORE THAN SHE'D like, but their continued resistance is exasperating. Mark finds himself solving problems for his daughter much more than he thinks is best. And Marie's solution to the sibling conflict problems in her home is to keep the kids apart. In all these situations, developing long-term strategies would better teach these children the skills they'll need for the future. An important part of your biblical philosophy of parenting requires that you invest now for the future.

Parenting builds patterns in children that will continue long past childhood. In fact, children are learning things about life, such as how to relate to others, solve problems, and handle emotions. The solutions parents employ now have the potential to help kids for the rest of their lives. Effective parenting requires a thoughtful, strategic approach, but, unfortunately, many parents don't have a plan. They just react to life situations as they come up. The alternative to having a long-term strategic plan is to engage in what we call *reactive parenting*.

Reactive parenting often gets the job done, at least for the moment, but it has a high price tag. Yelling at kids, for example, works to get them in the car or get the dishes off the table, but in the end, it doesn't teach kids the long-term skills and character they need. In fact, when parents yell at kids, three things happen. First, the child hears the message *I'm unloved, unworthy, and unacceptable.* Second, the parent/child relationship develops distance. And third, the parent feels bad, knowing that anger was an inappropriate parenting strategy and that negative long-term effects are likely.

The alternative is to think strategically about the present situation and about the future. The heart contains beliefs and convictions, and forms the tendencies a child has when faced with the same situation over and over again. For example, when a child reacts to frustration with an angry outburst, that's a heart issue. When a child steals some food and hides it in his room, the same is true. As daily situations provide opportunities for parenting, you can help your children develop the character they'll need to be successful in life. The parent who thinks long term approaches parenting problems with a different strategy and is much more effective. It's a matter of perspective.

A strategic approach asks different questions. Instead of just getting kids to clean up or be quiet, parents ask, "What heart quality is lacking here, and what are some ways we can develop that quality for the long term?" The question itself often reveals some different approaches and a more effective measuring tool for success.

When you stop to think about it, the problems children face now are the same ones they'll face when they get older. For example, a lot of adults whine, complain, have bad attitudes, and can't follow a simple instruction without an argument. So why not develop adult solutions for children's problems now, break them down to their developmental level, and practice the right response?

For example, Bill is thirteen and whines and complains about all kinds of things in life. Mom often gets irritated with Bill and, in exasperation, sends him out of the room. After a while Mom realized that Bill's problem is that he consistently communicates misery when he doesn't get what he wants. Instead of just getting angry with Bill, Mom now sees Bill's whining as a symptom of his focusing on a problem instead of a solution. "Bill, there are two kinds of people in the world, whiners and solvers. At the moment it looks like you're choosing to be a whiner. You need to go sit in the hall until you can think of something you're grateful for." After just two weeks of this firm approach with Bill, Mom saw significant improvement in her son. The difference was that she herself focused on the solution instead of just reacting to his problem.

Many children grow up to be adults with Bill's problem. They express their misery to others whenever they don't get what they want. A heart-based approach to parenting recognizes that behavior comes from the heart, and changes made now will produce lasting character later on.

One way to think long term is to continually ask yourself, "How is my approach to this problem helping my child develop the maturity needed for adulthood?" Be careful of the quick fix in parenting. It may get fast results, but what are you teaching your kids in the end?

Mary makes the mistake of thinking short term and uses reverse psychology with her three-year-old. "Don't eat your vegetables," she says playfully while she turns her back and walks into the kitchen. Her son quickly gobbles them up. She thinks she's winning the game with her son to get him to eat right, but in the end, she's encouraging disobedience. "Don't clean up the cars while I'm gone," she says, and her tot quickly plays the game. Mary is simply looking at the moment and believes she's successful because her son cleaned up the mess. Unfortunately, she's actually prompting her son to disobey her. Too many parents are like Mary, content with immediate solutions that have a high price tag for the future.

Roberto told us this story. "Sometimes I'd used sarcasm or teased my son when he made a mistake. I'd also yelled at him and demonstrated my disgust at his immaturity. And it worked. My son would respond to my challenges and make changes, but I began to see some side effects to my offhanded remarks. I realized that my son wasn't feeling like I loved him, and distance was developing in our relationship. It became clear that I was focusing more on the situation than on building confidence and maturity. I wanted to think more carefully about the way I was motivating my son to do the right thing. That realization changed the way I relate. I'm much more careful with my comments, measuring their long-term impact."

Even something as simple as learning to follow instructions teaches maturity. God has hidden within obedience the secret ingredients for success in life. When kids obey, they learn how to set aside their agenda for someone else, how to complete a job without Mom or Dad reminding them, how to report back when they're done, and how to be responsible when no one is watching.

Most important, while learning to follow instructions from Mom and Dad, children develop the necessary character to obey God as they grow older.

Parenting is a lot of work, but the time you invest now has benefits that will last a lifetime. After all, some of the most important qualities of life—like humility, obedience, respect, a good attitude, responsibility, cooperation, and honor—are learned in childhood. The daily interaction you have with children today can impact them for the rest of their lives.

The book of Proverbs reminds us that our present work as parents has long-term ramifications. It says, "Train a child in the way he should go, and when he is old he will not turn from it" (22:6). Your kids are in training now for the future. You are the coach. As you think about your child's future, the daily interactions of your family take on greater significance.

11

When your family is being pulled in too many different directions because of individual needs and interests, it may be time to focus on . . .

Teamwork . . . Individuals at Their Best

TAMMY IS FOURTEEN AND IS DOING WELL AT SCHOOL and with friends. Her parents are pleased. Her ten-year-old brother, Matthew, is on a traveling soccer team. Dad and Mom are helping Matthew develop diligence with his homework, and his grades are improving. They all attend church and are involved in a number of activities there. Each family member seems to be doing well, at least at the moment, but Dad and Mom feel that something is missing. They wish their family enjoyed their relationship together more. Somehow, it seems that the focus on their individual successes may be hindering their sense of family. These parents are wise to head off a problem early. Sometimes families get so focused on the achievements or challenges of the individuals, that the family itself suffers.

Independence teaches children important qualities, such as problem solving, confidence, and responsibility; however, it must be balanced with the ability to work on a team. Teamwork requires communication, compromise, and cooperation, essential qualities kids need for life. Children need to know what makes them special and unique, but they also benefit from seeing how a team approach to life's challenges produces great results. In fact, all life is mirrored in this careful balance of each person's assets versus the strengths of the group. Appreciating others and working together with them can often help the team do better than each individual working alone.

Imagine a soccer game where each player tries to score a goal personally and gain glory and satisfaction for himself. Obviously the game would be a disaster. Only through organization and cooperation can a team succeed. The same is true in a family.

When a sense of teamwork is strong, families do well. Individuals pull together to make things happen. It may be a day to clean up the yard, or a mission to care for a sick friend or relative. But when teamwork is demonstrated, individual needs are put aside for the success of the task or the good of someone else. Family members feel a sense of satisfaction when good teamwork results in success. "We did it!" may be the cheer at the end of a workday. "Together we can accomplish great things."

Teamwork is not always easy, especially if you have children who are rather competitive or self-focused. In that case, teamwork becomes therapy, working with kids over time to help them develop the heart qualities necessary to be good team members. It's often necessary to retrain family members to think about the goal and how to join in efforts to meet that goal.

In one family, Mom and Dad became uncomfortable with the lack of teamwork in their family. They saw each of their children plan individual events that they wanted to do. Pete, age twelve, wanted to play on the school baseball team. Karen, age ten, chose to join an after-school chess club. Micah, age six, began taking karate lessons. Mom and Dad felt like chauffeurs and social event coordinators for their kids.

The real downside, though, wasn't just the busy schedule; Mom and Dad began to see an individualistic mind-set that concerned them. Pete's friends and practice schedule began to take priority over his chores or time playing with his little brother. Karen's energies and time seemed swallowed up by classmates and school assignments. Although Micah enjoyed karate class, he often felt lonely at home and begged for playdates or TV time. Mom and Dad felt they were raising three individual young people who had very little relationship together.

These parents determined to make some changes. From then on, Sunday afternoon was family time, and that meant everyone was home. First they called a meeting to talk about the benefits of family. They talked about the treasure of having brothers and a sister growing up together and how one protects treasures. Then they laid out the plan. The first Sunday was game time. The next week would be a workday. The third week they did a puzzle together. One week they planned a family vacation. Although there was resistance at first, over time the sense of family teamwork grew and each member looked forward to those special times together.

This sense of teamwork does several things in a child's heart. First of all, it deals with some of the selfishness that's naturally resident there. Children must, on their developmental levels, learn that they have to put their needs on hold and act in someone else's best interest at times. This is often difficult for children, but so important for success in relationships throughout life.

Second, teamwork develops a sense of belonging. When I feel appreciated for my contribution to the group, I feel connected to others. This breeds security in kids and helps them develop confidence.

A third benefit of teamwork is the greater understanding of oneself. As I work side by side with my brothers and sisters, and my mom and dad, I begin to learn important things about myself and what makes me unique and different. When a child starts contributing to the team, that kind of service brings information to the table. Suzy is slow and methodical. She works with attention to detail. Paul is a big-picture guy. He can see the whole project and imagine what the finished product ought to look like. When a child enjoys the family as part of a team, he can even better enjoy who he is and what makes him special.

The Bible gives illustrations of families who lacked a sense of teamwork, and the results were disastrous. Some families, like Abraham and his two sons, Isaac and Ishmael, in the Old Testament, were torn because of disunity. When Isaac grew up, he didn't do much better than his father. Isaac and Rebekah chose favorites. Dad favored Esau, and Mom favored Jacob, resulting in their family splitting up. You'd think they'd learn, but then comes the story of Jacob and his twelve sons. Dad favored Joseph, creating more sibling conflict. A lack of teamwork in the family was passed on from generation to generation.

Paul wrote in Galatians 6:2–5 about the balance between taking care of your own business and also helping others at the same time. He said, "Carry each other's burdens, and in this way you will fulfill the law of Christ. If anyone thinks he is something when he is nothing, he deceives himself. Each one should test his own actions. Then he can take pride in himself, without comparing himself to somebody else, for each one should carry his own load." That's great advice for the church, and also helpful in the earthly family. Children can learn the balance with practice over time.

You may choose to call your family a team sometimes just to communicate the unity you share. When a job needs to be done, the "Smith Team" pulls together. You may work hard to clean up the house, or build a garden, or rake the leaves. Then you also have special privileges together as a family: going out to eat, playing games, or having ice cream.

Teamwork reveals itself differently in each family. In some cases it means all showing up at sporting events for the children, or working together on a paper route. In another it means guarding the dinner hour, requiring that the family be together at that time, making dinner a significant social event. The family enjoys unity as its members share activities, experiences, and common struggles.

One of the signs of a successful family is the ability to work as a team. If you see your family fragmenting or working more apart than together, it may be time to put some energy in this area of teamwork.

12

*When you evaluate all your tasks as a parent,
it's helpful to regularly go back and refocus by
looking at . . .*

Your Primary Responsibility

Try this. Ask your child, "Does God speak to you?" and then listen to the answer. It's amazing how many children don't realize that God wants to speak to them now. In fact, many children believe they'll be Christians only when they get older. That's too bad, especially given the fact that God's work in a child's heart is a strategic part of their growing maturity.

Of all the things you do in parenting, the most important job you have is to train your children to be disciples of Jesus Christ. The Bible is the guidebook for life, and when people, including children, follow it, good things happen. But how can you teach children about the Scriptures without making the process boring?

Some parents only use the Scriptures to correct their kids, giving their children the impression that God's primary task in our lives is to judge us. If your only use of prayer and the Scriptures is to correct your kids, you give your children the wrong impression about God. He is the one who also delights in spending time with us, affirms that we are his kids, and leads us every day. Those positive parts of our relationship with God should be communicated to children through family life on a regular basis. The use of God's Word in parenting is important, and here are some suggestions about communicating the message well.

First of all, you want your children to learn that the Bible is relevant. We're sure that you believe that the Bible is relevant to your life, but do your kids believe that the Scriptures are relevant for them? One of the ways you can help kids apply God's Word now is to end Bible stories with this question: "What's the lesson we learn from that story?" After all, telling kids a story about Daniel and the lions is different from telling the story about the three bears. The Bible is relevant. Psalm 119:105 says, "Your word is a lamp to my feet and a light for my path." Kids can learn practical lessons now that will impact their lives and lead them in their decision making. By discussing the lesson in the story, kids learn to apply the Scriptures at any age.

Another goal is to communicate to your children that the Bible is exciting. Devotions shouldn't be confined to the dinner table. Get kids running around, hunting for treasure, and solving problems. Remember that the language of children is activity. When teaching children spiritual truths, it's best to use their own language. A family devotion time should be the most fun time of the week. If you speak their language, they'll not only enjoy family time, but they'll beg for more.

Here's an example of a helpful activity and lesson. Cooperation and leadership in family life can be a challenge. Take the story of Moses and the burning bush and talk about some of the reasons Moses may not have wanted to lead the people of Israel. (What if he made a mistake? People would laugh. Maybe they wouldn't listen to him, he might not know what to do, etc.) Then play the "You be the leader" game in your family.

This game has three parts. In the first part, choose an activity and someone to lead. The activity could be cleaning up the kitchen after dinner, washing the car, raking the leaves, organizing the playroom, grocery shopping, or some other household chore. The leader could be Dad or Mom or one of the children. It's best to play this several times and change the leader.

In the second part of the activity, the leader leads the family to complete the task. This is often a challenge when a seven-year-old or fifteen-year-old is leading, but that's all part of the lesson. Don't break roles and take over the leadership.

When Dad isn't the leader, he could intentionally begin to argue and then catch himself and say, "Oh, I'm sorry. That wasn't honoring." When Mom isn't leading, she may begin to complain in a whiny voice. Actions like these add to the fun and become visual examples of problems that followers experience.

The third part of the game is the most important. Sit down and discuss the experience. Ask questions like, "What did you find difficult about leading? What did you find difficult about following? Do you prefer to lead or follow? Why? What makes leading easy? What makes following easy?" Use these questions to talk about your specific experience, but also discuss leading and following in general. Be transparent, and share some of the struggles you face. Then go back to the Bible story about Moses leading the Israelites in the wilderness in Exodus 3, and talk about the challenges Moses must have experienced.

After doing this activity, one mom shared that she'd prefer to follow but is often thrown into a leadership role. Dad, on the other hand, would prefer to lead in some situations, but he must follow because Mom is regularly involved in that area of family life. The young daughter shared how leading is made more difficult when followers complain or are uncooperative. Dad also talked about being a follower at work. Sometimes he needs to be a helpful participant and look for opportunities to encourage others to reach their goals.

Whatever you do, don't make devotions boring. The Bible is the most exciting book in the world. Not only does it contain role models in the form of heroes for all ages, but it also gives teens ethical dilemmas to discuss to help them hone their value system.

One dad told about the commentary on the book of Proverbs he created with his sons. Sheets of paper with headings such as "speech," "money," "listening," "discipline," and "guy/girl relationships" were all laid out on the table. Then as Dad read a chapter, the boys would identify any verses that could appear on one of their pages. They'd ask, "How does this verse apply to teens, the family, or to life in general?" They never published the commentary, but the process helped get the wisdom of Proverbs into the boys' hearts.

It doesn't take long to have a family time like this, but it does take some planning. Just twenty to thirty minutes a week of structured together time produces lessons that you can come back to over and over again spontaneously for months. The message you're teaching your children is that the Bible is exciting and relevant for their lives. That message, in their own language, will last forever.

13

With all the challenges parents face trying to help their children grow and change, one of the most effective tools is encouragement. Bring a positive dimension to your parenting when you . . .

BOOKMARK GOOD DAYS

"YESTERDAY WAS A GOOD DAY," LAURA REPORTED TO her friend Shelley at the park. "My kids seemed to cooperate more with me and with each other. I felt like I had a breather for a whole day. It was uncommonly peaceful."

Shelley's response surprised Laura. "Did you bookmark it?"

"Bookmark it? What does that mean?"

"To bookmark is to acknowledge the positive day with your kids. Point out the good you saw, and tell them how much you appreciate their cooperation and good attitudes."

Shelley's point is very important for any family. When things go well, don't just take the opportunity to rest up for the next problem. Be proactive and take advantage of the good day by affirming its importance.

There are things you can do on good days that you can't do on bad days. Good days are those days when a child is trying to overcome the weakness you've been working on. He's tried to respond better to instruction or is controlling his anger and not exploding when he doesn't get his way. At the end of a good day, you're encouraged, believing that there may actually be hope for a positive future.

Bad days are those days when kids resist you, don't cooperate with the plan, and seem intent on making the situation worse instead of better. Although we wish all days could be good, the reality is that sometimes a bad day is happening now and needs to be addressed.

You'll want to take advantage of the lessons that can be learned on both good and bad days. Because change comes in small steps, you'll often see some encouraging good days, but it's also likely that a bad day is just around the corner. So take advantage of the good day by providing a lot of encouragement and praise. You can acknowledge how positive you feel when your child is making progress, but be sure to affirm the growing character you see in order to encourage a positive sense of growth in your child. "Corey, I'm enjoying your compassionate heart." "Sharla, I know it's hard to be honest sometimes, and I can tell you're really working on it."

Kids sometimes can't see their own growth. After all, they don't have enough life experience to see that change happens. In fact, many parents are silent about progress and quite loud about deficiencies. Even in the midst of positive days, many children believe they're doing poorly. You might say, "Joan, I'm impressed with your ability to handle frustration today. It used to be that you'd quickly throw a temper tantrum, but now you seem much stronger in this area." Your affirmation on good days can bring hope to your child.

Proverbs 25:11 says, "A word aptly spoken is like apples of gold in settings of silver." A parent's encouraging words said at the right time can provide just the medicine for a child's heart. Some parents are quick with sarcasm, harsh words, or wit to "teach this kid a lesson." Remember that positive words of encouragement set the stage for growth in a child's life.

When you emphasize the positive, you're bookmarking that day. In the next few days, when things aren't going so well and a bad day seems to be developing, you can look back on that exceptionally good day and say things like, "Do you remember last week when we had that great day? You were really trying hard then, and we all felt better about life. Could you try to go back to doing the same things you were doing that day?"

Bookmarking good days gives children a memory to go back to. Remember, to create a bookmark, you have to express affirmation and encouragement in abundance on the day that things are going well. So, when things seem good, don't just sit back and rest up for the next challenge. Instead, take advantage of the moment and be proactive in affirmation and encouragement.

On the other hand, there are things you can do on bad days that you can't do on good days. Bad days are those days when your child isn't responding to the correction strategies you've set up. You're doing all the things you know to do, but your child is still not responding well. Sometimes on bad days, you as a parent can totally change your approach to see if another tactic may help. Other times, children are determined to have a bad day, and you, as a parent, must hold your ground. Don't try to sugarcoat a bad day by pretending it wasn't so bad. It was bad. Just go to bed and try again tomorrow.

Furthermore, on bad days children can learn an important lesson and end up saying to themselves, "I don't want to have bad days." That may seem obvious, but children who have a number of good days sometimes revert to previous negative behaviors because they forget how bad things were then. You may have to help your daughter see that a bad day is really bad and that the present choices determine the outcome. Your increased discipline is in direct response to the poor behavior.

Most of the time, bad days are followed by better days. Children don't like bad days any more than parents do. When a parent holds the line and makes a point by not giving in, kids get the message and make adjustments accordingly.

A child's bad day is tough on parents. You'll likely be upset a good portion of that day. Remember that if you're doing the right thing and your child is determined to resist, you're working to break down the stubbornness in the child's heart. Don't take your emotional turmoil out on your child. Just hold the line firmly.

If the bad days outweigh the good days, or if what you're doing doesn't seem to work, get help. Effective parenting requires steady growth. Just because you did all right with one child doesn't mean you'll do well with a second or a third. Children are all different, and they're always changing, requiring parents to be on the cutting edge of growth.

Parenting is tough. It takes a lot of work and continual learning. Look for ways to help children have good days. They need them, and so do you. Good days provide the footholds for hope to develop and a positive working relationship between parent and child.

14

It's disappointing to try your parenting ideas and find resistance from a spouse. Some parents get discouraged and give up, but . . .

Don't Minimize Your Parenting Power Because Your Partner Does It Differently

Vicky is discouraged. "I have all these ideas of what I want to work on with my kids, but my husband isn't on board. He doesn't see that they're important. He wants to do things differently." It's interesting that her husband, Fred, is also frustrated that his wife has ideas different from his. These parents both feel helpless and discouraged. Although it's encouraging when Mom and Dad share the same parenting philosophy and are working together, in reality it doesn't always work that way. In fact, your children have something to learn from each of you; so don't let differing approaches bring discouragement.

Of course, when at all possible, you want to look for ways to get on the same page with your spouse. Reading books, listening to CDs, or attending a parenting class together can provide opportunities to dialogue about values and develop plans for your child. Although raising children can be a great source of discouragement for couples with differing approaches, the opposite is also true. When parents work together and develop a plan to help a child grow up, their relationship as a couple can become stronger. Partnership builds unity, and parenting can provide that opportunity.

Unfortunately, though, some parents find such unity elusive. Parenting philosophies differ, and disagreements seem more frequent than agreement. The problem is that either values are dramatically different, or there's unwillingness on the part of one of the parents to grow in his or her parenting. Separated parents often find this frustrating because the conflict between the couple spills over to the child-rearing process. Some moms and dads struggle to work things out in their parenting approach because of other conflict in their adult relationship.

Single parents may feel discouraged by the lack of unity with the other parent when it comes to parenting. One dad said, "When the kids are with me, we have a bedtime. They are required to clean their rooms, and we don't eat junk food. When they're with their mother, she lets them watch R-rated movies, they stay up late, and they have poor eating habits." This dad is reasonably frustrated with the different messages the children receive. He knows, however, that he needs to emphasize convictions and values, not just rules, with his kids. After months of dialogue his daughter came home one day and said, "Dad, I did what you said and walked out of the room during the movie. I told Mom I didn't want to watch that movie they were watching." Dad beamed, realizing that his daughter was learning an important lesson about life.

Don't lose hope. Work hard to do the right thing, and hang in there. Your children need you, and your persistence will pay off in the end. It's amazing how much power one parent has. Although your efforts may be thwarted sometimes, keep working hard at your parenting and your kids will reap the benefits. Children watch how you live. They'll eventually have to make decisions about how they're going to live their lives. The key is to talk about the reasons behind your rules and why you hold the convictions you do. Children eventually see those reasons and are often persuaded by them.

Kathy put it this way: "I used to give up because my husband wouldn't support me even though I knew I was right. But I was seeing too many negative things happening, so I decided to be more firm even without his support. I wish things were different in this area, but I know that my kids need a mom who is going to be strong in order for them to make it in life. I've found renewed strength in knowing that what I'm doing is right, and although my husband isn't supportive, I take heart knowing that I'm pleasing God."

Sometimes it's not a matter of one parent doing right and the other doing wrong. Rather, they just have different parenting styles and either could be used to raise a child. For example, one parent is more relational and may let some things slide for the sake of closeness. Another parent values toeing the line to teach kids the right way to live.

Either of these approaches could work well, but trying to work them both at the same time can be frustrating for both parents. It's best, in those cases, to have regular parenting huddles. Sometimes you may do it one way, and other times you'll take a different approach. If parents are interested in cooperating, then the first decision is how to respond to the situation in question. The second decision is who should communicate the conclusion to the child.

Avoid having one parent be the bad guy all the time. If Mom is usually the strict one, then have Dad report the firm consequence sometimes. On the other hand, if the conclusion is to take a less strict approach, maybe Mom should communicate it. Working together like this can provide a sense of unity between parents.

When parents have different parenting philosophies or prefer to emphasize different values, the temptation increases to overemphasize your own perspective. Unfortunately, what happens is that parents then move further apart to compensate for what they believe to be a weakness in the other parent. This is a mistake. Rather, make an effort to understand the other parent and what values he or she is emphasizing. By learning to appreciate different parenting approaches, your relationship can become stronger. Recognizing differences and learning from them will allow your parenting to be most effective. Your kids have something to learn from both of you, so don't be discouraged by the differences. God can work through you both to touch your child's heart.

When parenting gets tough, remember Hebrews 12:1, "Therefore, since we are surrounded by such a great cloud of witnesses, let us throw off everything that hinders and the sin that so easily entangles, and let us run with perseverance the race marked out for us."

So, do what you can to compromise for the sake of unity with your spouse, but when that isn't possible, do the hard work of parenting. Your kids will be better for it.

15 *If selfishness in your children is hindering your family, it's time to . . .*

TEACH KIDS TO ADD ENERGY TO FAMILY LIFE

"I REALLY LIKE THE WAY YOUR BOYS GET ALONG AND look for ways to help out around here," Coach Chris commented to Tony as they cleaned up after the baseball game. "How do you get your guys to think about others and be willing to help?"

Tony smiled. "We certainly do work on that at home. It's a lifestyle we're trying to teach them. We call it *honor*. Honor has changed the way our family relates. Actually, our boys used to be quite self-centered, but we've worked hard to develop honor in our family."

Some children have the ability to suck the energy right out of family life. These kids are demanding of your time, need a lot of correction, and seem to be magnets for conflict. They're often emotionally explosive but almost always drain energy out of parents and other family members. Unfortunately, then, these children develop a negative view of themselves based on the high amount of negative feedback they receive.

One solution is to teach them to add energy back into family life. The term *honor* describes the process of thinking of others above yourself. Honor is important in a family. God commands honor to be practiced at home. Ephesians 6:2–3 says, "'Honor your father and mother'—which is the first commandment with a promise—'that it may go well with you and that you may enjoy long life on the earth.'" Those verses teach that honor learned at home has ramifications for life. In fact, we would say that God has hidden within honor the secret ingredients people need to be successful.

Honor has rich meaning for parents and children. It can give direction in many of the frustrating moments you experience. In fact, every form of selfishness has an honor-based solution.

Honor means to treat people as special, do more than what's expected, and have a good attitude. Feel free to use this definition or make up your own. The point is that honor changes the way parents relate to their children, the way children relate to each other, and the way children relate to their parents. Obedience gets the job done, but honor addresses the way people relate in that process.

If Jack gets people riled up each afternoon before dinner, set an appointment with him at 4:00 p.m. for several days in a row and ask him to look for three things he can do to add to family life. He may decorate the dinner table, encourage his brother, or prepare something nice for Dad's arrival home.

If Jack continually antagonizes his sister, try telling him that he needs to think of three honoring things to do for her before he's free to play. Remember, don't tell him exactly what he needs to do. If you decide what Jack needs to do and tell him to do it, that's obedience. When Jack chooses, it's honor. Honor treats people as special and does more than what's expected. Jack needs to learn how to add energy to family life instead of taking it away.

Honor requires initiative by adding something extra or doing something that needs to be done. Many children wait for others to tell them to do something. Furthermore, it's hard to teach kids to take initiative because the very act of telling them seems to take the initiative away. That's why you may require your child to do something but not tell him what to do. You want to help him start seeing a need or solving a problem for himself.

Honor carries the idea of going above and beyond. That means seeing what needs to be done and doing it, and solving problems instead of leaving them for others. One family had a sign in their kitchen that read:

> **IF IT'S BROKEN, FIX IT.**
>
> **IF IT'S EMPTY, FILL IT UP.**
>
> **IF IT'S OPEN, SHUT IT.**
>
> **IF IT'S OUT, PUT IT AWAY.**
>
> **IF IT'S MESSY, CLEAN IT UP.**
>
> **IF YOU CAN'T, THEN REPORT IT.**

That's honor.

Honor means that everyone contributes to family life. In fact, you may ask a child to go around the house and look for one job that needs to be done and do it, and then report back to you. These kinds of discussions and exercises will help children think outside of their little box and discover that they have a responsibility to the family. They can contribute to family life by just seeing something that needs to be done and doing it.

Honor has a tendency to diminish in a family because people tend to take for granted those to whom they're closest. It was Jesus who said, "Only in his hometown, among his relatives and in his own house is a prophet without honor" (Mark 6:4). The family can be a place where people take each other for granted. Learning honor is just the solution kids need. Hidden within honor are the secret ingredients that make people more productive in relationships.

You're already honoring your kids in a number of ways, though you may not be using the term. You might say to your daughter, "I went shopping today, and I bought your favorite ice cream. I just wanted to honor you." Then later you can use the same word to describe how you'd like your daughter to treat you with a better attitude when you give her an instruction.

One way parents can teach children honor is to include it in the instruction process. You could say to your child, "I'd like you to obey me by setting the table; then I want you to think of something extra to do to show honor. You choose; it's up to you. Report to me when you're done, and I'll check your work."

You can use the concept of honor in correction or when things are going well. You can use it when you teach your children about money, time, and other resources, and you can teach it when conflict comes around. One way to teach honor is on special occasions when someone wins a contest or earns a certificate. You may show honor by giving that person a fancy place at the table or by decorating his or her bedroom door.

Honor is fun. It's like oil in a machine. It gets work done with less friction and less heat. Every family needs honor. It's great when things are going well, and essential when family relationships are strained. Work on it whether your kids are preschoolers or teens. It'll change the way your family relates.

16

*If emotional intensity dominates family life,
you may want to consider . . .*

THE DIFFERENCE BETWEEN TASKS, PROBLEMS, AND CONFLICT

"WHAT KINDS OF THINGS MAKE YOU ANGRY IN FAMILY life?" asked Marvin, the small group leader. Several couples had gathered together for their weekly parenting support group. It was a good question and stimulated a lively discussion.

"I don't like it when my kids start fighting."

"I get angry when I have to say the same thing over and over again."

"Messes. I wish kids would clean up after themselves."

After several people shared, the group leader continued, "Today, we're going to learn how to reduce conflict. We may not reduce problems, but we'll reduce the conflict associated with those problems."

"What's the difference?" asked Sheri.

"That's the key question," Marvin replied. "In fact, in order to reduce the tension in family life, we have to understand the difference between three words: *tasks, problems,* and *conflict.*" Marvin's solution is a great one for any family. Here's what it looks like.

People develop patterns for handling the challenges of life. Some of those patterns are unhelpful, especially when they use emotions to attack the problem. Understanding the difference between tasks, problems, and conflict will bring insights into the solution and provide much-needed direction to your parenting philosophy.

Tasks are the normal things you do each day. You get kids out of bed, make sure they're dressed, provide breakfast, check that they have all the things they'll need for the day, and get out the door. Then you'll stop at the drugstore to pick up a prescription and drop by a friend's house to return a book on your way home. Tasks are the to-do list of a parent. They're work, but they're expected. It's part of the job.

The business side of family life requires that food be purchased, prepared, eaten, put away, and dishes cleaned up. Clothes need to get washed, folded, put in drawers, and then put back on people. Driving to various appointments, tidying up rooms in the house, and fixing things that are broken are all part of the business of family life. Every task between the time you get up in the morning until you go to bed at night requires effort. It's work. Those aren't problems. They're just tasks that need to get done.

Furthermore, training children is a task, not a problem. The difference has to do with your expectations. If you're surprised by your son's resistance to instructions, then you're liable to view it as a personal attack and escalate to conflict. But the reality is that your son's resistance is an indication of a character weakness. Part of your job as a parent is to train your child. Develop a plan to challenge the poor character in your son, and you then can accept the task of raising him, using a calm, but firm approach. It's just another one of the tasks of your job as a parent.

Problems are different. They're obstacles that get in the way of your goals. Your son is playing with his video game when he should be getting dressed. You can't find the prescription you need, and you just spilled coffee on your friend's book. Your daughter's homework isn't in her backpack again, and she can't find her other shoe.

It's not usually the tasks that create the tension in family life. It's the problems that get in the way. At that moment, you as a parent have to make an important decision. Are you going to move the problems down to tasks, or are you going to escalate them to conflict?

Here's an important rule: don't turn problems into conflict. Instead look for ways to turn problems into additional tasks by developing a plan to solve them and keeping your emotions in check. If more families would view problems as tasks instead of moving to conflict, then greater unity and more productivity would result. Unfortunately, many children and parents allow problems to turn into conflict so that most of the tasks of family life evolve into battles. You'll know that a problem is attempting to escalate into conflict when you hear a hurtful, sarcastic remark or an angry tone, or you see a disgusted look or a bad attitude, or simply see the intensity increasing between two or more people in a family.

Conflict happens when problems are met with emotional intensity. Mom yells at her son because he's playing with the video game. She rolls her eyes at her daughter and then sticks her neck out and points her finger as she angrily commands her daughter to look for her shoe and her homework. Mom has just raised the family threat level to red by turning the morning routine into an emotional experience.

Mom feels as though she's stuck in a common pattern. This isn't a onetime problem. It seems to happen every morning. Furthermore, the problem isn't limited to the first hour of the day. Things seem to get out of hand on a regular basis around her home. Mom doesn't like the fact that she gets angry, but she feels it's the only way to get her kids moving.

Part of the solution for Mom is to change the way she faces her day. If she'd move problems down to tasks instead of escalating them to conflict, she'd be much more at peace, and she'd reduce the tension her family experiences.

Compare two families as they respond to problems in their morning routine. With family #1, problems are a recipe for disaster, with yelling, dramatics, and tension flying around the room faster than anyone can manage. With family #2, parent and children work to find solutions to problems, minimizing the conflict as they proceed through the morning. Mom sees a mess that Shannon left in the bathroom. Instead of reacting with emotion, she calmly instructs Shannon to go back in the bathroom and straighten things up before coming to breakfast. When Mom finds Brenden playing instead of gathering his backpack and shoes, she confronts him and waits to see him respond. Mom's calm, firm approach focuses on moving problems back down to tasks.

The difference between the two families is that in family #2, Mom is committed to solving problems and reducing them to tasks instead of allowing them to escalate to conflict. But what do you do when children escalate problems into conflict? In that moment it's important for you, as the parent, to be on guard; you don't have to follow your child's lead. When kids generate conflict, it's important for parents to recognize the problem and move it down to a task. If a child persists and refuses to work on the problem without emotion, it's best for the child to settle down. Rarely is it productive to try to move forward to solve problems when emotional intensity is high.

One of the challenges we find is that parental expectations often fuel the escalation to conflict. Many moms and dads seem to believe that life should be problem free. When tasks are interrupted by problems, parents react with surprise and anger, when actually, problems should be expected. They happen. When parents learn to expect problems and develop the ability to turn problems into tasks, conflict becomes less common.

One of the greatest thieves of family closeness is allowing problems to move into conflict instead of keeping them as tasks. When family members work together to solve problems, they have a positive sense of accomplishment. On the other hand, conflict polarizes family members, causing them to feel like opponents instead of teammates. Ephesians 4:2–3 says, "Be completely humble and gentle; be patient, bearing with one another in love. Make every effort to keep the unity of the Spirit through the bond of peace." Your family can experience closeness together. That will happen as a result of intentional work in a number of areas, but one of the most important ones has to do with your ability to turn problems into tasks.

17

*Verbal battles between parents and children
often damage relationship. Therefore, it's
important to remember that . . .*

It Takes Two to Argue, but Only One to Stop

"Mom, can I go to the party at Sue's house on Friday night?"

"No, I'm not comfortable with Sue and her family."

"But her parents are going to be home. It's not a problem."

"I don't know them well enough."

"Mom, they're fine. They go to church just like us."

"That's okay. I still don't feel good about it."

"Mom, that's not fair. Just because you don't feel good about it, I get grounded."

"You're not grounded. You just can't go to that party."

"Why?"

And the dialogue continues, somewhere along the line turning into an argument and then into a fight. How can Mom stop the progression down this inevitable path? It seems to happen way too often.

Arguing can be defined this way: using logic and emotion to change someone's mind without considering how the intensity of the discussion is hurting the relationship.

The child who is prone to argue will often start with "Why?" in order to find ammunition. You, of course, view it as a harmless question, and since you have the answer on the tip of your tongue, you graciously answer it. The child responds with "But . . . ," and now you're both off and running. These kinds of discussions aren't bad (in fact, they can occasionally be helpful), but some children use them as manipulative techniques to get out of following instructions or to try to get something that you've already said no to. Arguing can become an irritating habit, but it's also a symptom of a heart problem.

Some parents try to talk their children into following instructions or have discussions to help them want to obey. These children can't follow a simple instruction without a dialogue and grow up to make poor team members, difficult employees, and demanding friends. Parents think they're doing a good thing. "After all," they say, "isn't it good to dialogue with your kids?" The answer is, "Yes, most of the time." However, there are some times in family life where dialogue is counterproductive. When children use the dialogue to delay obedience or try to wear you down in order to get a no answer changed to a yes, then you have a problem.

If you have a child who doesn't know how to cooperate, you may want to use a technique called "Obey first, and then we'll talk about it." This technique simply reverses the sequence of two important elements: discussion and responsiveness. Children must first respond to your instruction, and then you'll discuss the reasons for it.

Some parents who see a need for their children to give, not just take, require obedience by saying, "Because I'm the parent, that's why." Although these parents may have a handle on the problem, their authoritarian approach is inadequate because it focuses the solution on the parent instead of the child. Instead, challenge children that the problem is theirs because they're mishandling dialogue. A child may need a period of time where following instructions comes before the discussion in order to foster the ability to give up her agenda without always having to get something out of it.

When Amanda is asked to get on her pajamas and responds with, "But I'm not tired," Mom may say, "Amanda, you need to obey first, and then we'll talk about it." After Amanda obeys, then a discussion about bedtime can take place. It's surprising, though, how many children don't feel the need for a discussion afterward. Dialogue for them was simply an attempt to delay obedience.

Children who argue have good character qualities, such as persistence, perseverance, determination, creativity, and an ability to communicate their ideas. The problem with arguing is that your child views you as an obstacle, a mountain to tunnel through. The child who argues often lacks sensitivity, humility, and a proper respect for authority. Your challenge as a parent is to encourage the positive qualities and remove the negative ones.

When you sense that your child has crossed the line and is valuing his request at the expense of the relationship, stop the dialogue. Refuse to argue. Make it a commitment of your biblical parenting philosophy that you won't participate in this relationally damaging pattern. It takes two to argue, but only one to stop. If you refuse to engage, then you can stop the process from continuing on into unhelpful territory. Remember that good logic isn't the only consideration. You are also teaching your child to value relationship and learn to communicate in an honoring way.

One of the reasons that arguing is dangerous to a relationship is that it sets the parties at odds. When children argue with their parents, the relationship is at stake. Most parents feel uncomfortable with arguments, but they don't know why or what to do about it. The child who wants to argue puts the parent in an awkward position. The child takes on the role of attacker, and the parent then becomes the defender, or those roles reverse and the parent starts to attack and the child defends. This relating pattern sets the two up as opponents instead of partners.

The difference between an argument and a discussion has to do with relationship. When the issue becomes more important than the people debating it, the discussion has turned into an argument. The best way to teach, or even discuss a problem, is with you and your child on the same side of the net. Instead of allowing issues to come between you, look for ways to make the issue the opponent and you and your child partners in solving it.

Sometimes an argument can move into a discussion with a little adjusting on your part. If you believe a discussion is helpful in a given situation, move away from argument mode by asking, "What are you hearing me say?" or by saying, "Let's both try to think of advantages and disadvantages of you watching a video tonight." With these kinds of statements, you refuse to become an opponent and continue to look for areas of cooperation. The discussion then gives you an opportunity to teach problem-solving skills and good decision-making techniques.

Paul the apostle gave young Timothy advice about how to lead God's family, the church. In 2 Timothy 2:23 he said, "Don't have anything to do with foolish and stupid arguments, because you know they produce quarrels." That's not only good advice for the church; it's great advice for the home as well. Quarrels in family life often start with simple arguments.

One of the problems is that parents don't realize they're arguing until they're well into the discussion. That's understandable. The point you realize that you are in an argument is the point where you'll want to take action. Use the discomfort you feel with the interaction as a signal that it's time for you to make a change. Refuse to continue. After all, it takes two to argue but only one to stop.

18

When kids won't accept no for an answer and keep pestering you or whining about the problem, an important principle to remember is to . . .

MOVE FROM THE ISSUE TO THE PROCESS

CARLA BADGERS HER MOTHER. OVER AND OVER AGAIN she asks the same question. Mom says no to every request because she doesn't want to give in to the badgering. She explains numerous times to her daughter why the answer is no. Still Carla persists. Mom is tired of it, but she hangs in there with her daughter to show her that she won't give in.

Mom believes she's doing the right thing. In fact, refusing to give in is great. Unfortunately, responding to her daughter's barrage of arguments and complaints isn't working. In fact, giving reasons and arguing about the issue with her daughter seems to validate her dialogue. Mom would do better to leave the issue and move to the process.

The *issue* is the subject of the dialogue. It may be the dirty shirt, the video, or the snack. The *process* deals with the way kids handle the situation, the arguing, badgering, or whining. The child who brings the same request over and over again doesn't need more dialogue about the issue. The issue is closed. The child needs to be called to account for the way she's treating her mother.

Mom might say, "Carla, I've already said no to you. Do you see what you're doing? You aren't accepting no as an answer, and you keep pressing. That's the wrong thing to do. So, if you ask the question again or try to engage me about that issue, I'm going to discipline you." Mom is refusing to talk about the subject of their disagreement and instead is pointing to her daughter's poor approach. She's moved from the issue to the process.

Here's what's happening. As an adult, if you go to an authority and ask for something and receive a no answer, you usually have the freedom to ask one more time to clarify yourself or to further understand. However, if you receive a no answer a second time, then pushing further would be considered rude, crossing the line of what's socially appropriate. Children often don't know that line exists. They just keep pushing and pushing, and parents get frustrated, often ending the dialogue with an angry response.

You'll teach your children a valuable lesson about life if you'll leave the issue and move to the process. Instead of answering the "why" question over and over again, you may use the second or third "why" as a signal that your child is being demanding. When you say, "You've already asked that question and received an answer," you're drawing attention to the process, the way your child is approaching the situation. It's hard to correct a child for a desire to go over to a friend's house, but you can correct a child who is mistreating you in order to manipulate the situation. Children need to understand that the process is just as important as the issues of life.

Eleven-year-old George is disrespectful. When Mom says no, George uses sarcasm or a mean remark as he leaves the room. When Dad gives an instruction, George rolls his eyes or makes an offhand remark. Mom and Dad try to talk to George and explain why he needs to follow instructions or why Mom said no. George responds disrespectfully. Mom and Dad are frustrated because nothing seems to work.

George has a problem. His pattern of expressing his displeasure is inappropriate. He needs correction. But the focus of the correction needs to be on the way he's treating his parents. We gave them a plan for correcting disrespect. No more dialogue about the issue, but instead, move quickly to the process. The parents corrected for George's tone of voice, sarcasm, and poor choice of words and required a better response from him before moving forward.

This strategy began to work. It seemed that previously George found validation in the response from his parents that he wasn't receiving now. He'd developed some ingrained habits. That's all part of the process. When his parents continued to talk about the issue and disregarded the process, it actually encouraged George's disrespect. By drawing attention to the way George should respond, his parents contributed to a significant change.

By having a parenting philosophy that emphasizes the process and not just the issues, you can teach children many things. Kids learn to stop whining when they're unhappy, and how to bring a wise appeal when they get a no answer. You can help kids dialogue about conflict instead of using sarcasm or hurtful comments. You can motivate children to do a job with a good attitude.

Too many parents focus on the tasks, getting the job done, with little time spent on how they're getting those things accomplished. Focusing on the process opens up new avenues of teaching with your child.

In Philippians 2:3–4, Paul offered guidance to the church that's excellent advice for the family as well. He said, "Do nothing out of selfish ambition or vain conceit, but in humility consider others better than yourselves. Each of you should look not only to your own interests, but also to the interests of others." Later in that chapter, Paul continued, "Do everything without complaining or arguing" (v. 14). God is concerned with the process as well.

When a child is tempted to hurt others because of the issues, moving to the process by valuing the people involved may be just the parenting solution needed.

19

Some parents have a tendency to focus on the negative, not seeing the progress a child is making. If that's true for you, you'll likely want to look for ways to . . .

AFFIRM APPROXIMATELY RIGHT BEHAVIOR

ONE WAY TO KEEP A POSITIVE FOCUS IN YOUR DISCIPLINE is to look for *approximately* right behavior and affirm it. Don't wait until things are absolutely right.

If you ask your child to clean up the toys but find that he's only put away two things and left six out, you might say, "Oh, I see you put the blocks away. That's great! And I like the way you lined up your trucks! Now let me see you put the balls in the box where they belong."

By affirming approximately right behavior, you're encouraging steps in the right direction. One little boy was learning to dress himself, and Mom had a rule that he needed to be dressed before coming to the breakfast table. When he came downstairs with his shirt on backward and his shoes missing, she still praised him. He was trying. Pointing out his shortcomings would have been discouraging. He'd tried and was feeling good. Mom wanted to encourage his efforts.

If your teen is having a hard time finishing a homework assignment, you could be encouraging and point out how much she's done, rather than focusing on how much is left.

Imagine that your child is on a path from a weakness to a strength. If you spend too much time focusing on where your child is now, and point out the weakness, you make change more difficult. Rather, focus your words and your encouragement on the progress your child is making or on the destination or strength you're trying to build. Those comments go a long way toward producing internal motivation in your kids.

Some parents think the best way to motivate kids is to give them things as rewards. Those external motivaters are part of a behavior-modification parenting philosophy. Although they may bring about some change, there are many other stronger forms of motivation that come from the heart. One of those is the inner belief that I'm becoming a stronger person, or the desire to please God and others. As you encourage children about their progress and their focus on the goal, you'll be strengthening the internal motivation they'll need to continue on.

Paul affirmed approximately right behavior when he wrote in Philippians 1:6, "He who began a good work in you will carry it on to completion until the day of Christ Jesus." Paul was saying, "Be encouraged in the process, because God is still working in you." We give a gift to our children as we affirm them in process, not just completion. Remember that training takes time and implies lots of work. You're a coach, and your child is in training.

The reality is that everyone needs encouragement. Because children often fall short of expectations, many parents find it hard to make a positive statement. Sometimes parents think that if they give encouragement, their kids will slack off and feel that they don't need to keep working to improve. The reality is that encouraging children by pointing out progress can actually motivate them to hang in there and keep growing.

Growth is a process. It takes time. Character isn't developed overnight. Sometimes parents are motivated out of fear. They're afraid when they see weaknesses in a child that those deficiencies will dominate the child's character and end up ruining his life. Or, some parents correct because their children embarrass them, or they're afraid others may think they're bad parents. Fear has little benefit when it dominates parenting decisions.

Take time to ask yourself some important questions about your biblical philosophy of parenting. The person who allows fears to control parenting has a hard time living with children who are in process. Annoyance, defiance, or lack of cooperation in kids results in major trauma for parents. Those weaknesses are important, and parents need to take firm action, but being firm and reacting out of fear are two different things.

As you influence your children to develop the qualities necessary for success in life, take time to point out how far they've come. "I notice that you're responding much better to disappointment now. Do you remember how you used to yell and scream when you didn't get your way? We haven't had one of those episodes in a long time. I'm proud of you. You're growing up, and I'm liking the person you're becoming."

In the same way that focusing on character gives parents perspective as they develop strategies, emphasizing how far children have come on the path toward that character provides emotional strength to continue. That encouragement is necessary for kids, but it's also helpful for parents as they think about their children. Be careful about overemphasizing weaknesses, or you may talk yourself into disliking your child.

If you take time to emphasize how far your child has come and the progress made over the years, you'll be encouraged by the person your child is becoming. That's what real love is all about. It's interesting to read 1 Corinthians 13:4–7 through the eyes of a parent. "Love is patient, love is kind. It does not envy, it does not boast, it is not proud. It is not rude, it is not self-seeking, it is not easily angered, it keeps no record of wrongs. Love does not delight in evil but rejoices with the truth. It always protects, always trusts, always hopes, always perseveres."

One of the greatest ways to learn how to love is to have children. It's then that we learn to love others in their uniqueness. We want to help them change, yes, but love keeps a healthy balance between who they are and where they're going. When parents learn how to love, great things happen in them and in their kids. Of course, love takes time. Love is demonstrated in the process, not just in the perfection.

20

When you know what your kids need to do, but they're not doing it, you may be tempted to use anger to solve the problem. In those moments, remember that . . .

It's Not Good Enough to Be Right—You Also Want to Be Wise

"He deserved it," said Charlie after he chewed his son out for backing the riding mower into the car, leaving a large scratch along the fender. "If he'd just pay attention to what he's doing, this wouldn't happen. He just doesn't think sometimes."

Charlie had spent considerable time teaching his twelve-year-old son, José, how to handle the mower. In fact, Dad took pride in the fact that his son could handle this piece of equipment better than most kids his age. But Charlie mishandled José's mistakes. Continually yelling at his son weakened José's willingness to try new things and risk making mistakes. Yes, Charlie is right. His son needs to pay more attention to what he's doing. But Charlie's response was unwise. It's not good enough to be right. You also want to be wise.

Parents often use the fact that they're right to justify poor parenting responses toward their children. In fact, most people who unleash their anger at others believe that they're right, and often they are. Kids fall into the same problematic thinking. One nine-year-old boy said to us, "If you had an annoying brother like I do, you'd beat him up too."

When people develop a justice mentality toward life situations, they justify their revenge and anger. A biblical parenting philosophy doesn't just focus on being right, but also looks for the wise response. A wise person recognizes when he's right and then chooses the best course of action to bring about the desired change.

Ken worked hard with his daughter Alisha to get a homework assignment completed, but Alisha forgot to turn it in the next day. Ken was angry. He'd gone to all that work to help his daughter, and she didn't even turn in the work. Ken took a deep breath to settle himself down before he went in to confront his daughter. Instead of blowing up at her, he expressed sadness and disappointment in her lack of responsibility. He took away the privileges his daughter was planning for the evening and required a phone call at lunch the next day to report that she'd talked to the teacher, apologized, and turned in the assignment.

Alisha needed correction, but she didn't need an angry tirade from her dad. Wisdom requires insight, alternate solutions, and the ability to hold back damaging emotions in order to offer helpful strategies.

In the heat of the moment, an angry response may seem justified. When a person feels he's right, he somehow also feels empowered to release his frustration because "the situation warrants it," or "the person deserves it." The next time you feel angry because your child did the wrong thing, take a moment and ask what your goal is. If you're just trying to get revenge, then anger becomes the weapon of choice for most infractions. If you're trying to help your child grow or change, then anger rarely does the job. That's why James 1:20 says, "Man's anger does not bring about the righteous life that God desires." You may be interested in helping your child do the right thing, but anger is a poor tool to accomplish it.

Taking a moment to focus on your goal can mean all the difference. When you're in a disagreement with your teenager, you likely can win the argument by overpowering the situation with better reasoning or emotional intensity. But if your goal is to change your son's thinking, consider taking a different approach. Sometimes strategic quiet or thoughtfulness can lead a young person to explore a new idea more thoroughly and allow him to come to a new way of thinking. And then you've accomplished your goal.

Moving your child out the door in the morning is only a secondary goal. The primary objective is to teach responsibility and time management. Getting good grades at school isn't the most important thing. Rather, you want to teach thoroughness and perseverance in the process. By focusing on the heart quality, you'll likely choose a more strategic response. Rarely does that come with a focus on being right.

Pause for a moment and ask, "Why am I angry? And what would be the wisest way to handle this situation to maximize change?" Just a few minutes' pause can bring clarity back to the situation, and give you the wisdom you need to move forward most effectively.

Marsha told us this story. "I came into the room and couldn't believe what I saw. My ten-year-old daughter was painting her school project on the dining room table. I wanted to scream at her. What was she thinking? At the same time I had the presence of mind to realize that she was being responsible with her assignment and trying to make it look great in order to get a good grade. So, I took a deep breath, and asked her to put the brush down and come into the kitchen. I first affirmed her initiative with her schoolwork but told her that I was afraid that she'd damage the table. I told her that I'd like to help her move the project outside onto newspaper on the picnic table. I was able to teach her about the danger of paint on our table while at the same time encourage her about doing a good job on her project. If I'd have exploded, like I felt like doing, then I'd have lost the teaching opportunity."

Kids need discipline. They need to be corrected. They're young and immature. But many parents move too quickly to correction strategies that are harsh, instead of those that are most effective. We're not suggesting that you be lenient with your kids. On the contrary, a biblical parenting philosophy recognizes that firmness teaches character, but the way you approach the situation can mean all the difference between whether the correction is accepted, resulting in change, or resisted, resulting in continued foolishness.

Be careful that you don't use the fact that you're right to justify unhelpful responses or exaggerated consequences. A lot of parents are right. Few are wise. It's wisdom that maximizes growth in kids.

21

USE FIRMNESS TO FOCUS ON CHARACTER

"MY DAUGHTER DOESN'T GET IT. I TRY TO BE NICE TO her and say yes whenever I can, but sometimes I have to say no, and then she treats me like I'm the enemy. Furthermore, I feel like I can't correct her because then she gets mad at me. I want to have a close relationship, but I can't do that and be a parent at the same time. I'm afraid I'm going to alienate her. I don't know what to do."

Sometimes parents are afraid to be firm with their kids for fear that their kids won't like them or that they'll add too much pressure that their children can't handle. Unfortunately, many children take advantage of their parents' graciousness and don't reciprocate in a positive way. The reality is that many children need a boot-camp experience in following instructions, working on attitude, or getting control of their anger. Firmness is an important parenting strategy.

Firmness makes a child's present pattern of response uncomfortable. It's amazing how comfortable some children are with resistance, whining, meanness, or bad attitudes. Firmness makes it clear that we aren't going to continue to live this way. Some parents immediately think of consequences when they think of firmness, but consequences are only a piece of the strategy. One of the things that makes firmness work is clarifying expectations. When you write it down, post it on the wall, or simply ask your child to repeat what you expect to happen, you're reinforcing your firm approach.

Another aspect of firmness is constructive confrontation that uses the power of words without anger to give further clarity to the situation. Getting close to a child and saying, "Lee, I feel like you're not obeying me. I asked you to stop watching the video and come and help me in the kitchen. You need to turn it off now." Anger isn't necessary, but your close proximity increases the discomfort the child is experiencing. When a child doesn't respond to your relational approach, firmness communicates that change isn't optional.

One way to demonstrate firmness is to wait expectantly once you've given the instruction, expecting the child to start moving toward completing the task. When you give a child a job to do, don't just walk away and assume it'll get done. Your child may need for you to stand there for a few moments to make sure he's moving in the right direction. Your firm presence at that moment increases the anticipation and moves children forward.

Sometimes parents have a parenting philosophy that moves too quickly to corrective strategies and overuses the toolbox of consequences. Remember that all consequences weaken in their effectiveness over time, so, when possible, it's best to rely on other tools, such as firmness. Constructive confrontation, waiting expectantly, and clarifying expectations are all important for establishing a firm parenting approach and often work before consequences become necessary.

Be careful, though, that you don't just focus on what your child needs to stop doing. Focus on what the child needs to do instead. In fact, it's best to focus on a heart-quality or character issue. "Mindy, we're working on kindness, and what you just did to your brother missed the mark. So, I'd like you to try that again. Show me some kindness."

Character is often learned under pressure. It's true that life imposes its own pressure on our lives, but sometimes kids can't feel it. That's when parents must help them feel the pressure a little more. We aren't suggesting that you be mean to your kids, but it's often helpful to apply strategic pressure at times so kids can strengthen areas of weakness.

The home is a place for children to learn and grow. If kids don't develop self-control, cooperation, honor, and integrity at home, they'll have a much more difficult time out in the world. In fact, your controlled firmness at home can teach children lessons more easily than the harshness of life that will come later.

Romans 5:3–4 reads, "We know that suffering produces perseverance; perseverance, character; and character, hope." The important principle in this passage is one that applies to all people, even children. Growth often takes place under pressure.

Notice that there are four words in that verse: *suffering, perseverance, character,* and *hope*. When parents increase the pressure (suffering) and give kids a plan (perseverance), then growth (character) is the by-product, and a positive view of the future (hope) is the result.

A biblical parenting philosophy has a focus on character and demonstrates a willingness to add some suffering, in the form of firmness, into a child's life. Essentially you're going to communicate the message, "We aren't going to live this way anymore. This isn't good for you now or for your future, and it's not good for our family." Your strategy is to help your child feel uncomfortable with the present operating plan. Things have to change. Firmness starts moving kids in a positive direction.

But don't just start being firm without giving your kids a plan of what you want them to do. Focus on the character quality you're trying to develop. If your son resists instruction, you're going to work on cooperation. If your daughter is mean to her brother, then she needs to practice kindness. If you have a child who lies, then integrity is the goal. If you keep your eyes on the positive character needed to move forward, you'll be able to maintain a positive approach even in the midst of the pressure you're creating.

One of those words in Romans 5 is, again, "perseverance." Your child needs to develop it, but few children understand what perseverance is. Kids tend to live for the present and often want things immediately. Adults know that many good things take time and hard work, and children will need to develop perseverance in their lives in order to be successful. If you're developing a plan for kindness, then help your child know how to persevere. When her little brother is annoying, how should your daughter respond? What does kindness look like? When your son wants to finish the video instead of helping you in the kitchen, how should he think differently about the situation? Answers to those kinds of questions help children know what perseverance looks like in very practical terms.

Once you've clarified the goal (character) and you've given your child a plan (perseverance), then you add the firmness (suffering), and good things start to happen. The beauty of this approach is that kids not only start to change but they experience the hope promised in the verse. They begin to believe that it's possible to get a good grade when they work hard, or handle their emotions when they develop self-control.

Using the Romans 5 model for helping children change negative behavior patterns gives both parents and children a road map for addressing difficult parenting challenges. Not only do the children experience more hope, but the parents do too. Firmness is a good parenting approach when it fits into the greater goal of character development. Instead of just telling kids what you want them to stop doing, you'll be challenging them to work toward a goal and to move forward toward maturity.

22

When change in your kids requires a lot of correction and pressure, be sure to keep in mind that . . .

Children Can Only Take as Much Pressure as the Relationship Will Allow

Dale, a father of two teenagers, gave an insight-ful illustration that applies to parents of children of any age. "When I'm working around the house, I know that to unscrew something or open a lid, I turn to the left. If I want to tighten it, I turn to the right. I wish it were that simple with kids. Do I tighten up with them, or do I loosen the reins a bit? I want to have closeness, but I also want my kids to grow. Those seem to be opposite directions sometimes, and I'm left paralyzed, not wanting to make a mistake." That's a great observation, and answering it will help you add a significant piece to your biblical philosophy of parenting.

Children need correction and discipline. Their immaturity often requires that you take firm action. We're advocates of firmness and setting tight boundaries for children in their areas of weakness in order to teach them how to live differently. Discipline, however, must take place in the context of relationship. When the pressure must increase for a time in family life, be sure to also increase times of fun, affirmation, and closeness. The two must go together. Too many parents fail in this area, viewing themselves simply as disciplinarians. Emphasizing relationship in your biblical parenting philosophy becomes the difference between a family and the military.

It's important that children learn respect and responsiveness to authority, but that doesn't mean that parents have to be demanding and harsh to teach these qualities to their children. Let's take the example of giving instructions to kids. Sometimes parents forget about relationship. They see something that needs to be done and yell out commands to the kids to do it. Dad walks into the kitchen and sees the trash overflowing and yells, "Jimmy!"

It's not enough to see the need and tell someone to respond to it. That approach doesn't demonstrate value for the relationship. Parenting isn't just about getting tasks done; it's about building relationships at the same time. If Dad were to take a moment and look for his son, he may find him having a meaningful dialogue with his older sister. The instruction might best be postponed a few minutes.

On another occasion when Dad wants to give an instruction to Jimmy, he might find him at the computer and take an interest in the game his son is playing before giving direction. Firmness doesn't have to be cold and distant. Eye contact, gentle words, and extra time can add a personal touch to parenting that helps children feel valued. Putting your hand on your son's shoulder, calling your daughter close to give an instruction, addressing a child by name, and speaking softly are all ways to show children that they're important.

Of course, sometimes children need to drop what they're doing and follow instructions. That's part of learning obedience. Many kids can't seem to follow an instruction without an argument. In those situations your child is likely going to need some practice at giving in and doing the right thing without a dialogue. But your firmness in those moments can still be done in an honoring way.

Like every step in a good instruction routine, getting close to each other requires changes from both child and parent. Children also find it tempting to yell across the house. They need to learn that dialogue only takes place when relationship has been established through eye contact and being physically close together. Sometimes it's the small things that demonstrate that a parent cares or that a child is willing to listen. Putting down the paper, looking up from the computer, or just turning to face your child before you speak communicates the importance of your relationship together.

Children and parents should be friends, but don't let that desire weaken your limit-setting. One mom of three teens said, "I used to feel bad when I had to say no because I thought they'd be mad at me. Now I've learned to make a decision and enforce it because it's the right thing to do. They may get mad, but I have to do it because I'm their mom. After they settle down, they know I did it for their own good."

Maintaining a balance between firmness and relationship is essential for good parenting. If you find yourself erring on one side or the other, you'll see negative symptoms in your children. The parent who overemphasizes relationship may find that a child takes advantage and doesn't respond properly, resulting in patterns of arguing, resistance, or complaining. On the other hand, the parent who continually orders kids around loses the closeness that the relationships provide. View the symptoms as warnings to readjust your approach in order to keep the balance in place.

Parenting mistakes happen in even the best homes. You don't always have to be right. Having a strong relationship with your kids helps everyone deal with the regular challenges, mistakes, and uncertainties of maturing together. Peter reminded us of that when he wrote, "Above all, love each other deeply, because love covers over a multitude of sins" (1 Peter 4:8). That truth is so important for the family. Disagreements happen, emotional energy rises, and tension fills the air at times. What's going to save the day and preserve the situation? It's the relationships you develop with those fellow family members. When love increases, it's much easier to resolve conflict and get through the challenging times.

Learning how to love in a family is important. It's more than just the hug at bedtime. Love happens even in the challenges we face. What does it mean to be loving when you have to discipline a child, say no to a request, or require a child to separate from something she's involved in to follow an instruction? Paul gave some helpful words of advice in Colossians 3:12: "As God's chosen people, holy and dearly loved, clothe yourselves with compassion, kindness, humility, gentleness and patience." Those aren't the opposite of getting things done, correcting kids, or staying on schedule. In fact, those words illustrate for parents ways that they can add relationship to their parenting.

Strong relationships with children often serve to decrease their resistance to your leadership. A firm but loving approach reveals to children that you not only have expectations but you are also supportive and caring. Furthermore, relationship is the conduit through which values and convictions are passed. Since one of your goals is to pass your faith on to your kids, you'll want to have a strong relational foundation to make that happen.

Sometimes a gracious approach in a parenting philosophy is perceived as weakness. It doesn't have to be that way. Usually graciousness just adds a bit more time to the process, allowing relationship to envelop the tasks that need to get done. When parents demonstrate love in the midst of their parenting, kids learn important lessons about life. Life can be hard sometimes, but love can reign in the midst of it all.

23

Correction is part of your job. But to do it effectively you'll want to understand . . .

THE DIFFERENCE BETWEEN PUNISHMENT AND DISCIPLINE

DIANE'S FAMILY WAS HEADED FOR TROUBLE, BUT SHE couldn't see it. Here's what she said: "We have three kids under the age of nine. We want to make the expectations clear for our kids, so we put up a chart on the refrigerator to spell out consequences for every offense we could imagine. We listed the offenses commonly seen in our home and then told the kids what the punishment would be."

Unfortunately, Diane is on a fast track to damaging her family. Here's why: she doesn't understand a fundamental principle, and she needs to add this to her biblical philosophy of parenting in order to be successful in raising her family.

Diane needs to understand that there's a significant difference between punishment and discipline. Punishment gives an unwanted consequence, but discipline means "to teach." Punishment is negative; discipline is positive. Punishment focuses on past misdeeds. Discipline focuses on future good deeds. Punishment is often motivated by anger. Discipline is motivated by love. Punishment focuses on justice to balance the scales. Discipline focuses on teaching, to prepare for next time.

Jesus didn't have any kids, but he had disciples. The words *disciple* and *discipline* come from the same root. The goal of parenting is to disciple your kids in what it means to live life. This training comes in several ways: modeling, instructing, talking, practicing, and even correcting. The problem is that many parents lose their positive approach when it comes to correcting their kids.

The reality is that correction is one of the ways kids learn. So parents need to have an attitude toward correction that keeps discipling in mind. The child who teases relentlessly, the one who whines for a snack, and the one who bickers with his brother all have one thing in common: a need to adjust behavior patterns and change the heart. Some parents only use condemnation or anger to motivate their children to change. This attitude says, "If I just point out the problem enough times, he'll eventually change." Or, "If I give him enough consequences, then the punishment will make him want to change."

Unfortunately, the negative approach that punishment often takes is counterproductive, weighs heavily on the relationship, and often hinders forward progress. What these kids really need is firm correction with a positive focus. That means focusing on what your children should do to replace the negative behavior. It takes more work to discipline instead of punish, but the rewards are worth it. Children develop new patterns, and relationships grow stronger.

You may be saying, "Yes, I know that my parenting philosophy is supposed to be positive, but how can I be positive when my kids are doing the wrong thing?" One way is to state rules and requests in positive terms. Instead of saying, "Don't shout," say, "We talk quietly in the store." Instead of, "Stop being rough with the dog," try, "Be gentle." Instead of complaining about the clothes all over your four-year-old's room, you could say, "You need to put your clothes in the hamper when you take them off."

Some parents protest, "That sounds great, but my kids don't listen. They need something else to get them to change." And we would agree that most children need a multifaceted approach, not just words. But through it all, you'll use words, and we suggest those words be positive and encouraging.

Eleven times the book of Proverbs advises children to listen to parents. For example, Proverbs 1:8 says, "Listen, my son, to your father's instruction and do not forsake your mother's teaching." If kids are supposed to listen to their parents, it must mean that parents have something to say. Your words are important. Don't abuse the listening ears of your kids by yelling words of condemnation and revenge. Use your words strategically as tools for heart change and character development.

Sonia has four kids under the age of seven. She carried around a clicker on her arm for a day. She clicked down once for every negative statement and up once for every positive statement she made to her kids. Sonia was surprised at how many times she communicated even positive things in a negative way. So, she went to work to change her vocabulary. She looked for ways to affirm her children and to say things in a more positive manner. Instead of, "No, we're not having a snack right now," she said, "Yes, you can have that as a snack at three thirty this afternoon." An interesting thing happened that Sonia didn't expect. The atmosphere around her house began to take on a more positive attitude. Her kids seemed to accept her comments more readily, and relationships improved.

It may take some work, but clearly stating or restating a directive in positive terms gives your child a clear picture of what you expect and keeps your interaction on a positive note. Give gentle reminders to point your kids in the right direction.

Of course, many children need more than just a positive way of talking about their weaknesses. They require correction, but the way you correct can mean the difference between resistance and responsiveness from your children.

Ephesians 6:4 says, "Fathers, do not exasperate your children; instead, bring them up in the training and instruction of the Lord." The first part of the verse describes a negative way of relating to children. *Exasperate* gives the impression of being harsh and causing discouragement. In place of that negative response, fathers are instructed to do something positive: bring their children up in the training and instruction of the Lord. You don't want to discipline your kids to simply get rid of negative behaviors. The purpose of discipline is to train children and show them a better way to live.

Many of the problems children have are either behavioral habits or character deficiencies. It would be nice if they could have a "burning bush" experience that would change their lives instantly, but it usually doesn't happen that way. Even Moses had to spend forty years in the desert as a shepherd leading sheep before he was ready to lead God's people.

Change takes time, and many small corrections and reminders can contribute to long-term growth in your child. The word *discipline* used in the Old Testament is translated from the Hebrew word *chanak*. It means "to train." Training implies guidance to a particular goal. Every day you're training your children to become healthy, responsible adults.

It's easy to get upset when your children need a lot of correction or when they don't seem to change. Some problems take longer to overcome than others. Your response is important. Exasperation can damage the relationship.

When parents understand and embrace the difference between punishment and discipline, it changes the way they relate to their kids. Instead of giving a consequence to balance the scales of justice, they look to teach and to train. Instead of viewing discipline times as annoying detours on the path of life, they see them as opportunities to further develop character in their kids. A small change in perspective can make all the difference.

24

Children often act out at times and in places where it's hard to graciously discipline them without creating some kind of scene. If that happens regularly, then

DON'T PRACTICE IN THE GROCERY STORE—THAT'S THE FINAL EXAM

"WHAT DO I DO WHEN MY KIDS ACT OUT IN PUBLIC?" That's the most commonly asked parenting question. It's frustrating when children throw tantrums, run away, whine, complain, or disobey in the grocery store or at church. It would be nice to have a little booklet titled *How to Parent in Public* that you could not only use for yourself but also pass on to others who are caught in the drama.

The answer is that you don't practice your discipline strategies in the grocery store. That's the final exam! You practice in the kitchen, bedroom, laundry room, and backyard. Children need to learn how to handle disappointment at home so they can accept a no answer in the checkout line. Kids who haven't learned how to accept correction at home without a bad attitude will miserably fail the test when they have an audience.

Children develop patterns of relating. They're predictable. Maybe when you say no to your four-year-old, she's likely to have a temper tantrum, or when you give an instruction to your eight-year-old, she'll argue with you, or when you correct your thirteen-year-old, he blames the problem on others, including you.

At times, parents feel as though they're caught in a dance, and they don't know how to turn off the music. They know that things shouldn't happen this way, but it's hard to make changes. These patterns are called *relational routines*, and they become more ingrained over time.

Negative relational routines are most embarrassing when you're in public. While at the soccer game, your son begins to argue just as he does at home. At church, your daughter reacts to you with the same disrespect you've been seeing for weeks. These public arenas aren't the place to practice changing relational routines, at least not until you've done significant homework.

Children's tendencies to relate in particular ways develop over time and often require concerted effort to change. Once you identify the specific problem, then practice doing the right thing over and over again.

For example, Ricky, age four, ignores his mom when she gives him an instruction. She has to say the same thing several times, often with increasing intensity, before he responds. Mom decides to work on the instruction routine with Ricky. She realizes that part of the problem in their pattern is that she gives Ricky instructions while he's still involved in his task. Mom decides to change the pattern and determines not to give instructions to her son until he's broken concentration from his activity. In fact, Mom explains to Ricky that from now on she's going to just call his name and expect him to come. Ricky won't know why Mom is calling him. It may be because it's time to go out the door, or time to have a snack, or just because she wants to say, "I love you."

Mom then begins the homework by practicing this new "Come when you're called" rule with Ricky. Most of the time he comes, but sometimes he doesn't, resulting in immediate correction and more practice. Mom affirms Ricky for his responsiveness when he comes. Once she has him close and gives an instruction, she sees marked improvement in his obedience. Mom continues to practice the new routine with Ricky several times a day. Then she practices at the park and around the neighborhood. When she feels confident that Ricky has changed the relating pattern significantly, Mom tries the new routine at the store or at church, with encouraging results.

Gary realized that his teenage daughter was disrespectful to him in front of her friends. He'd seen the same sarcasm and unkindness when they were alone, but it was particularly disturbing in front of others. Gary knew that although the "public" routine matched the "private" routine, the embarrassment was greater with an audience. Gary didn't want to just look good in public, however, so he began to change the way he and his daughter related in private.

When Gary sensed that his daughter was being rude, sarcastic, or unkind in their discussions, he'd stop the dialogue with a statement such as "That wasn't kind" or "You don't have to treat me unkindly because we disagree." In some situations the comment was enough for his daughter to snap back into healthier dialogue. On a couple of occasions, though, his daughter was particularly angry and refused to back down. Dad required a break from the dialogue to settle down and even told his daughter that she needed to stay off the computer and even out of her bedroom until she was willing to talk to him about the problem in a mature way.

After working on the relating pattern for a few weeks, Gary found himself again receiving disrespect in front of his daughter's friends, but this time he was ready. Gary called his daughter out of the group into the other room and confronted her. She received the correction in part because of the homework that he'd done the preceding weeks, and she knew he was serious about the change.

Patterns take time to adjust and often require that parents focus on relational routines. The next time you're frustrated with the interaction you see from your child, stop and consider whether it's a pattern. If so, try to figure out what the triggers are that get it started. Next, identify some new ways of relating, and then practice them over and over again until they become the new habit.

The English word *instruction* is composed of the words *in* and *structure* and basically means "to put structure into." When someone comes on the scene and gives instructions, that person brings structure to the situation and helps people know what to do. Mom sees the negative relating pattern between two children and gives guidelines on how to interact in a more positive way. She adds the structure needed at the moment to make family life work. Unfortunately, because of the well-worn relationship between parent and child, kids may react with resistance. That's because the habits are built over time and need concentrated effort to change.

Hang in there. Remember that you're not giving instructions about how to relate simply to make life easier. You're helping children develop healthy relating patterns for the future. Without clear guidelines about structure in relational routines, family life falls apart. Instruction doesn't just mean telling kids what to do, though. It means practicing the right way to relate over and over again.

Ephesians 6:1 says, "Children, obey your parents in the Lord, for this is right." Parents don't require obedience because it's convenient; it's the right thing to do. Practicing the right thing over and over again helps children develop patterns that will help them forever.

25

If your kids tend to resist, then you need a plan. So . . .

Be Prepared for the Three Arenas of Resistance

SOMETIMES PARENTS GET OFF TRACK BECAUSE THEIR child's resistance surprises them. It's as if they expect their child to say, "Thanks, Dad, for saying no to that movie. I really appreciate the limits you set for me." Or, "I appreciate it, Mom, when you make me clean up my room and make my bed." If you expect your children to always appreciate your discipline, then you're going to be frustrated, feel unappreciated, and take resistance personally.

Kids don't often appreciate discipline when they're growing up. Many times the gratefulness comes when they're adults or when they eventually have their own kids. To persevere every day, parents must have an internal confidence that they're doing the right thing. Those who feel uncertain or are always second-guessing themselves can end up feeling confused and overwhelmed. These feelings can lead to frustration and anger toward the kids. Of course, the poor parenting strategies that result from anger further complicate the situation, and parenting problems get worse.

Being mentally and spiritually prepared for parenting challenges can mean all the difference between progress and setbacks in a child's growth. This may seem obvious, but many parents take their kids' reactions personally. One dad said, "When my son is disrespectful toward me and doesn't listen, it reminds me that people often don't listen to me at work either. Even growing up, I didn't feel like I received much respect from people. So when my son treats me this way, it brings back all kinds of memories, and I end up with a poor response that makes things worse. When I realized that I was reacting to things from the past and that my son doesn't have all this history, I was able to respond differently. I'm the parent. I need to do my job. It's a much more freeing position for me as a parent."

Disciplining kids is hard. It's frustrating at times and difficult both for the child and for the parent, but kids need it. The hard work of parenting produces results, although those results might not seem apparent immediately. Hebrews 12:11 says, "No discipline seems pleasant at the time, but painful. Later on, however, it produces a harvest of righteousness and peace for those who have been trained by it."

Resistance usually requires correction. Unfortunately, it's easy to view correction as a detour on the path of life, and most parents don't plan for detours. They're eager to get the job done or get where they're going. Correction is an interruption to the work of family life. It can then quickly become an irritation and frustrate even the best of parents.

Resistance from children often happens in one of three arenas: when given an instruction, when corrected, and when given a no answer. In fact, some children have a problem in all three areas. When it comes to following instructions, for example, many children don't like to be interrupted from their play. They want life to be easy. Many kids believe their primary job in life is to have fun. Consequently, your instructions get in the way. Part of your task is to teach children that their primary job is to learn to obey and follow instructions, not just to get things done or to make life easier for you. Family life is where children learn valuable lessons about work, relationships, and giving up their agenda for someone else. Heart qualities of cooperation, flexibility, and responsiveness to authority are learned when parents teach their children to follow instructions.

The second area where resistance is common is during correction. Kids often don't want to admit that they're wrong or accept responsibility for their part of the problem. They blame the problem on others, rationalize their actions, or defend themselves so they don't have to look at their own guilt. That resistance is a sign of immaturity, and your persistence in the face of resistance teaches children that correction is part of life. In fact, many of the lessons of life are learned through correction. It's a tool God uses to teach young and old alike.

When children learn to respond well to correction, they learn humility, responsibility, and how to handle guilt. When children respond poorly to correction, they're missing out on one of the ways that God provides growth and training.

The third arena of resistance is when a child is given no as an answer to a request. When kids can't have what they want, they sometimes become demanding, disrespectful, and belligerent. Some kids resort to badgering or whining when they don't get their way. Children need to accept no for an answer, and one of the jobs of parents is to teach children that lesson by being firm. By learning to accept no as an answer, kids learn contentment and graciousness. Furthermore, they learn the spiritual skill of living within limits and they'll be able to say no to temptations in life.

If parents can learn to anticipate resistance, they can better prepare themselves to remain calm but firm. Sometimes the resistance is an indication of something else going on and requires a listening ear. The parent who is surprised by opposition can easily resort to anger in order to overpower the child into submission, missing a valuable teaching opportunity.

Don't let a child's poor response dissuade you from what you know is best. Remember that your job isn't only to help your children be happy. You also want them to grow and mature. That sometimes means experiencing the pain of wrong choices or the disappointment of a no answer. Allowing children to experience the discomfort of discipline can be a very loving thing to do.

So, when you need to discipline your child, and get a poor response, remember that discipline isn't intended to be fun. Although you want to look for creative ways to teach and make learning a joy, sometimes, to learn a lesson, a child needs to experience a negative consequence. Anticipate resistance by being prepared, and persevere because you know that what you're doing is best for your child. The discipline is a valuable part of your child's growth.

When your children are having a hard time accepting correction, remember that their immediate response isn't an indication of the effectiveness of the discipline. You are disciplining for long-term benefit. This truth can help you persevere. It can be quite freeing when parents recognize that because discipline is unpleasant, children often won't respond with gratefulness. Sometimes parenting isn't easy, but discipline is a necessary part of the job.

26

Kids tend to gang up on you or feed off each other when you try to correct them together. You'll find it more productive to . . .

DISCIPLINE KIDS SEPARATELY FOR SIBLING CONFLICT

"HEY, GIVE IT BACK."

"I had it first."

"No you didn't. I had it first."

"Stop it!"

"Moooom!"

And of course, that's your cue to go in and try to play Solomon and come up with some wisdom when your children are fighting or bickering.

One of the saddest things for parents is sibling conflict. You know the possible long-term negative consequences of the fighting, teasing, and bickering between your kids. You want your children to have close relationships, but it seems that they're determined to undermine any unity by their negative interaction.

One mom told us, "When the bickering gets too bad, I just go in my room and shut the door!" In fact, many parents believe that the solution to arguing and teasing is to allow children to "fight it out."

Other parents, to maintain peace, separate the children and try to keep them apart. They imitate a referee at a boxing match, breaking up the conflict and sending the fighters to their opposite corners. Unfortunately, continually separating children doesn't solve the problem. In fact, inevitably the bell rings and the children come back to fight some more.

Both separating children and letting them fight it out are inadequate solutions to sibling conflict because they lack the depth needed to bring about lasting change. When parents only separate the offenders or walk away, they miss valuable opportunities to help their children grow.

Conflict between brothers and sisters is a child's first class in relationships. Your home is the classroom, you are the teacher, and a healthy plan for working on conflict is the curriculum. Each conflict situation becomes an opportunity for teaching children how to relate more effectively.

One of the most important strategies for addressing sibling conflict is to discipline the children separately, not together. Kids have an amazing way of deflecting discipline when they're together—ganging up on you!

When two children are fighting, call one out of the room and talk about how to deal with the conflict. Some parents feel that they must stop everything and administer consequences to both kids in order to parent effectively. A better response is to train them in the moment. By removing just one of the kids, you're able to help that child develop better conflict management skills. When your son complains that you're only disciplining him and not his sister, then use it as an opportunity to do some teaching. You might say, "I'm disciplining both of you, but you each need a different approach. You're right that your sister needs correction, and I'm going to help her with that. But for now, her immaturity is a great way for you to learn how to handle conflict more appropriately. That's why I'm training you."

Teach children how to confront, ignore, negotiate, compromise, talk about problems, affirm others, and be peacemakers. And when they've reached a point of frustration, rather than lash out, they need to get help, typically from you. Send the child back into the situation to try again. You may call the same child out of an activity five or ten times in an hour to continue to point out the change that needs to take place. Help children know what right actions are appropriate, and as long as they're willing to try to do the right thing, send them back into the situation to practice. If necessary, call the second child out and give helpful suggestions as well. Coaching in this way can equip children with the skills and strategies they need.

The reality is that each child needs individual help to deal with the selfish sibling and with his or her own selfishness. By working with each child separately, you gain tremendous influence over the process, and you can accomplish much more.

Recognizing that sibling conflict is an opportunity for relationship training gives the problem a whole new perspective. As you listen to your children's interactions, you'll be able to identify specific skills they need, buttons that are easily pushed, and relating weaknesses that need to be addressed.

Of course, when children come to you with a problem, you'll want to avoid the "he said, she said" dialogue. Many kids want to discuss who started it and who had it first. The real question that helps kids deal with conflict issues is, "How could you have handled this in a better way?" Or, "What can you do to make this situation work?" Certainly there are times when parents must step in to discipline one or more of the kids, but many times kids practice conflict resolution skills with a little guidance from a parent.

Often it's helpful to acknowledge the immaturity of the other child: "You're right. Your brother shouldn't be hoarding all the pieces. He's wrong and needs to be corrected. But yelling at him and pushing isn't the right way to handle it. Let's talk about what you could do to resolve this problem in the best way." Kids need training. The reality is that the same problems often come up over and over again. Children need a plan, and then they need to practice it.

One time two guys came to Jesus to ask a question, revealing their competitive nature and their own selfishness. They wanted the best seats. In Mark 10:37–44 James and John asked Jesus if they, not Jesus' other friends, could sit on his right and on his left in his kingdom. The question reminds us of many kids who compete with one another for the best seat or the first place in line. That competitive nature simply reveals selfishness. Jesus' answer to his disciples is instructive for all of us, and particularly helpful for children. He said, "Whoever wants to become great among you must be your servant."

Most children need help knowing how to deal with their own selfishness and with the selfishness of their brothers and sisters. As you work with your children in this area, you're preparing them to deal with life. After all, adults face challenges with selfishness on a regular basis. The lessons learned now will be used for the rest of their lives.

27

Angry children tend to instigate fights. When your child baits you, look for ways to . . .

AVOID THE BOXING RING

TWELVE-YEAR-OLD JASON WAS ANGRY. DAD HAD MADE it clear that this Saturday they would work together to clean up the yard before the evening barbecue, but Jason wanted to go canoeing with his friend. All morning Dad looked for ways to foster a sense of teamwork, but Jason resisted, offering jabs here and there about how unfair it was that he had to spend his Saturday working in the yard. "My friends don't have to do slave labor on *their* Saturdays."

Dad tried to be patient and understanding, but by late morning he had had it. Why couldn't Jason just cooperate and stop acting so selfishly? Dad's anger began to grow inside. It wasn't long before angry words filled his thoughts. This scene could have turned quite ugly, but then Dad remembered the Boxing Ring principle. With a quick prayer he was able to settle his heart and plan a different approach to the problem.

Dad took a quick break to go inside and get two cold drinks and a snack to share with his son. He then went back outside and called his son over to take a break. The discussion that followed began like this, "Son, I know you're upset about having to work today, and disappointed about missing the canoe trip, but we have a significant problem here with your attitude. If you can't make a change in the way you're treating me, then I'm going to have to discipline you." Dad wasn't willing to allow his son to continue on the present course, but he was also committed to disciplining his son without fighting with him.

When children are angry, they try to bait parents to join them by fighting, being unkind, and using intensity. It's as if the child is in a boxing ring, taunting the parent to come into the ring and fight it out.

Of course, many moms and dads know they have louder voices, better fighting skills, and greater intensity than the child, so they willingly step into the ring. That one decision to fight anger with anger causes parents to miss tremendous opportunities. As we discussed in an earlier chapter, yelling at kids creates damage in three areas. First, children receive, and start believing, the message that they're unworthy, unacceptable, and unloved. Second, the relationship develops distance, with each anger episode creating another brick in a wall between parent and child. Third, the parent, knowing that anger is the wrong response, ends up feeling guilty, and rightly so.

James 1:20 says it well: "Man's anger does not bring about the righteous life that God desires." There's a better way, but many parents tend to believe that anger represents strength, and anything less is a sign of weakness. That belief distorts their parenting philosophy and keeps them entrenched in an anger pattern, instead of freeing them to look for better solutions. A firm approach is necessary in many cases, but anger is not. Strength isn't measured by one's ability to pour emotional intensity into a situation. Rather, godly strength is demonstrated by remaining under control, yet still being able to proceed through the minefield of conflict in relationships. Only the most mature are able to move forward through a conflict situation without losing their cool.

Once parents develop a strategy for better parenting that reduces their own anger, they'll still have to fend off their children's angry responses. Kids don't like to be angry alone. They want company. So they send out invitations to their anger party by pushing parents' buttons to draw them into the ring. It's surprising how many parents

RSVP and say, "I'll be right there." Then they join their kids in the anger episode.

Children are smart, and they know which buttons will set Mom or Dad off. It's amazing, though, how many parents take the bait. A child may say, "You never let me have a snack," and suddenly the parent is ready to fight. Or he says, "Dad wouldn't do it this way," or "I don't want to go to school," and Mom goes into a tirade. Children often know that screaming or kicking the wall will provoke a parent. If you find those opportunities irresistible, that may be an indication that you need to do some work on your own anger.

James 1:19 says, "Be quick to listen, slow to speak and slow to become angry." That's certainly needed advice for parents. It's amazing, though, how easily parents get sucked in. When surveyed, most parents say that they get angry when their kids get angry. It's a common response, but that doesn't mean it's helpful.

Angry children need to see that the anger is their problem. When parents jump into the ring, then the focus is taken off the offense, off the child's anger, and a new problem is created in the relationship. By remaining calm and firm, you're able to help your child address his own anger.

Another problem is that children who grow up in explosive homes learn to make decisions based on avoiding the next angry outburst. Unfortunately, they then may grow up to be people pleasers, trying to keep others happy instead of making decisions because something is right or wrong. Instead, children need to learn how to make decisions based on values and convictions. How do they do that? They learn, in part, when parents discipline with firmness and love instead of anger.

Some parents seem quite content with a parenting philosophy that uses anger to solve parenting problems. After all, anger often works, at least in the short run. It gets kids moving or motivates them to stop and listen. But in the end, it does damage to a child's decision-making ability. Children often need firmness when they're out of control. Parental intensity doesn't need to be part of the equation.

"So," you might ask, "how do I keep calm when my kids lose it?" The answer is that you need a plan. People who don't have a plan often use anger to solve problems. When it comes to parenting, the lack of a plan results in using anger as a consequence. Anger may appear to be an easier solution, but remember, you aren't parenting simply for convenience. At least you shouldn't be. You're parenting for the long term. When you take the extra time to develop a plan for real heart change, children grow up with the tools they need to be successful in life.

The first part of the plan is to refuse to enter the ring. "I'm not going to fight with you," you say. "You need to go sit in the hall and settle down." Sometimes it means you must walk away for a bit. Of course, children who want to fight will try to woo you back into the ring. Refuse to play that game.

Next you'll want to develop some solutions for the various parenting issues you face. Identify those areas where you tend to get angry, and work on new strategies for addressing those particular problems. That may take some work, but if you have the plan in place, then when you start to get angry, you can calmly move into your plan.

It takes some strong character and self-control to respond calmly in the face of anger. For a while you may just want to put extra effort into remaining calm when your child's upset. Instead of focusing on discipline or solutions or getting kids to do the right thing, it may be most effective for you to make your primary goal to remain calm. You'll be surprised at the long-term benefits for you and your child when you learn to stay out of the boxing ring.

28

*Emotions such as anger, disappointment, excitement,
or anticipation can quickly create challenges in
family life, so it's valuable to . . .*

TEACH KIDS TO COMMUNICATE
EMOTIONS WISELY

THE GRAND GEYSER IN YELLOWSTONE NATIONAL
Park is the largest, most predictable geyser in the world. It usually
erupts every 8 to 12 hours, with eruptions lasting about 12 minutes. Although the eruption is spectacular, it's not as predictable as
Old Faithful, the most well-known geyser in the park, which erupts
every 35 to 120 minutes and lasts fewer than 5 minutes. People stand
around, waiting with anticipation for the next eruption. The whole
process is a reminder of many families, where eruptions can take place
at any time.

Every successful family needs to have a plan for addressing emotions, so they don't get out of hand. One of the key indicators of
maturity is the ability to manage and communicate emotions in a
healthy manner. Most parents find themselves frustrated with their
children's emotional outbursts and don't know how to respond themselves without getting emotionally involved. A sign of a healthy family
is an ability to manage emotions well. That doesn't mean that each
person always demonstrates self-control; it means that family members understand how best to respond to their own emotions and to
those of others.

Emotions aren't bad, but sometimes the actions that come from those emotions can be hurtful. Empathizing with the feelings without condoning the actions can be a challenge for any parent. Here are some suggestions for developing emotional maturity in kids.

First of all, children who are emotional by nature need to learn that their heightened sense of emotion is a gift that needs to be developed and managed, instead of viewed as a curse to be tolerated. The emotionally sensitive individual has the ability to pick up on cues in the environment faster than others. This person can often walk into a room and see that something's wrong before others can. God has given an extra scoop of emotions to some kids, and they may eventually become pastors or counselors because they can learn to understand the emotions of others as well. Or maybe your child will become a good salesperson, able to sense the best time to close a deal. The point is that kids' emotional reactions, though needing correction, are often a sign of a strength that simply needs to be managed.

There's a difference between emotional sensitivity and emotional reaction. Kids can learn that anger is good for identifying problems but not good for solving them. After all, Jesus got angry, but he knew how to use his anger in a productive way. Mark 3:5 says, "He looked around at [his enemies] in anger and, deeply distressed at their stubborn hearts, said to the man [with a shriveled hand], 'Stretch out your hand.' He stretched it out, and his hand was completely restored." Jesus didn't react out of his anger. Instead he turned it around and did something productive. Children can be like Jesus in this same way, but it takes training. Unfortunately, many children simply react to their emotions, resulting in hurtful words and actions. There's a better way, and the home is a great place to learn it.

Most children need to develop greater awareness of their internal emotional state. Some kids don't know that they're angry until they've broken something or yelled some mean words. They need to see their anger coming on before the reaction in order to be most productive. One of the ways to help children recognize their own emotions is to observe emotions in others. One dad wanted to work on emotional awareness with his seven-year-old daughter, Diane, who seemed oblivious to her own emotions and those of others. He used a journal and, in the evening, asked Diane to identify examples of a friend or family member who was sad, glad, or mad that day. Then he asked, "How might you respond to that person in a helpful way?"

They continued this exercise every evening for two weeks. After a while it helped Diane get outside of herself, look at the needs and feelings of others, and then talk about ways to respond appropriately. When her brother is mad, it may be best to leave him alone or to just ask a helpful question. With her friend who is sad, she could offer to help and then listen empathetically. When Mom is glad, Diane could enter into that gladness by listening to the story and enjoying the situation too.

Knowing how to communicate emotions is also important. Some kids are internal processors, churning away but not letting others easily see their struggle. Others are external processors, revealing everything they're thinking to anyone who will listen. Kids benefit when parents talk more about emotions and the various types of feelings they experience. Whether they're embarrassed, sad, afraid, or disappointed, kids often respond with anger, not recognizing the other emotions that are present. Parents can do significant teaching by reflecting the emotion that they see. "It looks like you're disappointed that you can't go to the soccer game. That makes sense. I'd be disappointed too. But that doesn't mean you can treat others unkindly."

Again, children don't recognize that they're upset until after they've hurt someone or said something inappropriate. For example, the child who doesn't like an instruction or limitation may reveal frustration outwardly, sometimes in a small way and other times with downright revenge. Help her recognize her frustration *before* she acts out.

One mom said, "I can tell when my thirteen-year-old son is having a bad attitude. He becomes more abrupt in his actions and words. His roughness sends a message that says, 'I'm not happy with you.'"

By making observations earlier, Mom was able to raise the awareness level in her son before the explosion took place.

It's important to remember two rules of engagement when confronted by a child's anger. Rule of Engagement #1 is, don't be afraid of your child's emotions. Sometimes children use outbursts as a form of self-protection to prevent parents from challenging them. In that case, you need to view the display of emotion as a smoke screen, and look past it to the heart of the issue.

You may choose not to confront in the heat of emotion, but don't let your child's anger prevent you from correction. Parents sometimes see the emotion as a personal attack and react to it, losing any real benefit that could come from the interaction. That brings us to . . .

Rule of Engagement #2: don't use your own anger to overpower your child's anger. Proverbs 15:1 says, "A gentle answer turns away wrath." When you begin to lose it, take a break. Come back later and work on it some more: "I've been thinking about the way you responded to me earlier when I asked you to do your homework. I'd like to share an observation that might be helpful for you. It seems that you believe you ought to be able to wait and do your homework just before bed or in the morning before you go to school. Is that what you're saying? One of the values I'm trying to teach you is that self-discipline often means we work first and play later. That's one of the reasons I require you to do your homework early every day. I'm trying to teach you an important value. I know you may not agree with me, but I want you to know why I'm asking you to do homework before dinner." Further consequence or correction may be needed, but allowing the emotion to settle before the confrontation may help the child be more receptive to the correction. And it's not just the emotion of the child that needs to settle. Sometimes the parent needs a bit of time to return with a wiser approach.

Allowing emotions to settle first can bring opportunities for dialogue later instead of turning the present issue into a battleground. Realize that kids will go away thinking about what you've said, even if their initial response looks as if they haven't heard you. Prepare what you're going to say and choose your timing carefully, without getting caught up in the emotion of the moment, and you'll help your child learn to deal with emotions more appropriately.

29

When you find yourself giving the same instruction to your child over and over and over before you see responsiveness, maybe it's time to . . .

STOP TALKING AND START ACTING

"ABBEY, TIME TO PUT THE DOLLHOUSE AND DOLLS AWAY."

"Abbey! Did you hear me? It's time to clean up."

"Abbeeey! It's bedtime! I told you to stop playing and start cleaning up."

"*Abbey!* You need to obey. It's time for bed. Put those dolls away now!"

"Abbey, I mean now! Why don't you listen to me?!? *You need to clean up now or I'm going to . . .*"

How does your child know when it's time to get moving when you give an instruction? How does she know when you mean business? The answer is, because you give cues, and your child knows what those cues are. The solution to delayed obedience is to tighten your *action point*. Every parent has an action point. An action point is the point when you stop talking and start acting, or the point when children know you mean business. It's a biblical parenting philosophy demonstrated in practical terms.

Think back on your own childhood. How did you know when your dad or mom meant business? Maybe they used your middle name or started moving toward the kitchen where that special utensil was kept. They may have gotten out of the chair or started moving toward you or given you that look. The point is, you knew.

Action points differ among adults. Dads have a different action point than moms. The teacher at school and the babysitter each have an action point, and the way children respond is determined by the cues those leaders give.

Unfortunately, many parents use anger as the cue that tells their children it's time to get moving. Although it may work in the short run, the harshness has negative side effects. An important skill in parenting is communicating your action point without anger.

Perhaps you're saying, "But my kids won't obey unless I get angry." You're probably right, but only because you've taught them to wait until you're angry before they have to respond. Your cue is anger, and your kids know it. If you find that you've been relying on anger to motivate your children, it's time to make a change. What signals do you want to use to indicate that it's time to clean up, or it's time to go?

You might say, "Karyn, please turn off the TV now." The child's name and the word *now* can become the cues that the next thing you do is follow through and take action. Or you could preface what you're going to say with the words, "Karyn, this is an instruction."

When you're ready to make the change, talk with your children. Explain that you've been unwise in teaching them to wait until you get angry before they start obeying. From now on you're going to ask them once; then comes the action. If your child doesn't respond to the new cues, then move right to a consequence.

Be careful of multiple warnings or counting to three, as those strategies can weaken the instruction process. One warning may be helpful to make sure the child has understood the instruction, but then the next step should be to follow through. If you tighten your action point, you'll get angry less frequently, and your children will respond more quickly.

Many parents are afraid of becoming like a sergeant, ordering their children around and expecting instant obedience, so they become so relational that their instructions sound more like suggestions, ideas, or opinions. Or, they believe they have to talk their children into wanting to obey. That's an example of a poor parenting philosophy.

Many children in those homes, then, can't seem to follow even the simplest instruction without a dialogue. If this pattern continues, these children tend to make poor employees, develop selfish attitudes about following someone else's leadership, and have a difficult time in relationships because they haven't learned how to sacrifice their own agenda for others.

Explaining reasons behind instructions can be valuable at times, but sometimes even we, as adults, must obey first and then understand later. God asked Abraham to sacrifice his son without full understanding and then considered it faith when he obeyed (Genesis 22:1–2). Peter didn't know why he was to go to Cornelius's house but went anyway, only to discover that God wanted to bring salvation to the Gentiles (Acts 10). Philip was asked to leave a revival in Samaria and go out into the wilderness, not knowing why; but when he got there, he led an Ethiopian man to Christ (Acts 8:26–40). The point is that children don't have to know the reason why in order to respond to an instruction.

Some parents are hesitant to teach their children responsiveness to authority because they don't want their kids to blindly obey just anyone who says something. Challenging authority is not wrong, but it's an advanced skill, and children first need to learn how to give up their own agenda and cooperate with others.

A common problem parents experience is keeping kids moving in the mornings. One mom developed a new morning plan, and this is how she shared it with her nine- and eleven-year-old children: "I've been doing a lot of yelling in the morning, and I don't want to do that anymore. So here's the plan. We're going to have checkpoints each morning. At 7:15 a.m. you need to be down for breakfast, all dressed with shoes on, and your bed made. By 7:50 a.m. you need to have completed your chores and combed your hair. Those are the checkpoints.

"I'm doing this to help you manage yourselves each morning.

You're old enough to do that instead of relying on me to keep you going. You'll feel better about the morning, and this plan will reduce the tension we usually experience. To help you be motivated to meet these checkpoints, I want you to know that if you miss one checkpoint in a morning you'll have to go to bed a half hour earlier that evening, since you must need more sleep in order to get up and get yourself ready."

They ended the meeting positively, as the children felt empowered and eager to manage themselves the next morning. Mom's plan took some extra effort and work to enforce at first, but in the end, the morning routines went more smoothly. Her children were successful at getting ready, and Mom didn't have to nag or be harsh. She replaced yelling and nagging with firmness. The checkpoints helped define her action point, and the children understood the new guidelines.

A child's quick response to parents has spiritual ramifications as well. It's always best to respond to the whispers of the Holy Spirit in our hearts. But when we don't listen, God may have to use other ways to get our attention. There's no better time than now for children to learn this valuable lesson about life.

30

*Kids sometimes can't accept your no answer
and look for all kinds of strategies to get you to
change your mind. It's not wrong to change your
mind, but be careful that you . . .*

Don't Give In to Manipulation

When your child doesn't get what he wants,
what is his response? Sadness is reasonable. But some kids resort to
angry outbursts and manipulative techniques that are immature and
unacceptable. Emotional outbursts, dramatics, and whining are habits children sometimes engage in to try to get what they want or to
simply make others miserable.

Saying no to a child's request can be one of the most difficult
of all parenting responsibilities. You may wonder if you're being too
strict, or you may second-guess your decision because your child
seems so upset. The process of saying no is complicated by a child's
ability to use a host of manipulative techniques to get you to change
your mind.

Children may not even realize they're being manipulative. They view
themselves as pursuing a goal. In fact, many parents mistake demandingness in their child for the good quality of perseverance. One mom
told us, "I like it that my son keeps coming back to me. He's persistent."

Unfortunately, many children don't realize when they've crossed
the line from persistence to demandingness. That line is crossed when
children value their issue more than the relationship. When a child
yells at a parent or says unkind things because he doesn't get what he

wants, he's crossed the line.

Parents who use simple behavior modification in their approach to demandingness often use distraction to help children change their minds. As a discipline strategy, distraction offers something equally or more attractive to the child to motivate the release of the original request. This approach often works and can even be a good part of a biblical parenting philosophy, but if it's the only response, then children start evaluating options based on their personal value instead of learning how to accept no as an answer. Sometimes parents who overuse distraction as a parenting strategy end up with children who continually want to play "Let's Make a Deal," or the whole experience feels like negotiating with a terrorist. The reality is that sometimes children need to accept no for an answer because the answer is no. It's the ability to live within limits. Contentment is a godly quality and it's taught at home.

A child's demandingness has many forms. Badgering, arguing, whining, dramatics, the silent treatment, and passive resistance can all be unfair tactics used to change a parent's mind.

Sometimes badgering is simply an attempt to gain attention, and lots of it: question after question after question. Some children seem to have the strategy down to a science. But parents can be just as determined. One mom tried so hard to resist her son's badgering that he finally threw his hands up in frustration and said, "Mom, you can be so stubborn!"

Any parent who has a child who badgers feels the unending tension in the relationship. Parents may want to hide, or even look for ways to avoid their son or daughter. Some parents say they cringe when they see the child coming into the room with those eyes of determination. The tension in the relationship has become a real irritation.

If you have a child who doesn't know when to quit, you'll first need to point it out so that your child becomes more aware of the problem. You might say, "Son, we're back in the badgering routine here. I want you to stop now and not ask me for anything else for the next hour. We can continue to talk or be together, but no more permission questions for a while."

Sometimes older children will ask questions or make statements to try to convince you to bend rules. One favorite question is, "What's wrong with it?" A young person may come to Dad and ask to go hang out at the mall, or at a friend's house after school, or attend a party on Friday night. What's wrong with those things? Nothing, necessarily. The wise parent knows, however, that it's often in those situations that bad things begin, but the child just can't see it. It doesn't seem reasonable.

It takes a pretty committed parent to stick to a no answer in a questionable situation, and many fail. "Well, I guess you could go to that party, and hang out after school at your boyfriend's house" and . . . pretty soon things happen that change the course of the child's life.

"What's wrong with it?" is a question that misses the point. It's like creating a soup. We're not just throwing things into a bowl. We don't say, "Well, there's nothing wrong with this dirt. It's actually clean dirt, so we'll throw it into the soup." Rather, we handpick the ingredients to make the soup nutritious.

Don't allow your children to convince you to make changes you know aren't in their best interest. Furthermore, don't let them use manipulation to get what they want. Habitual manipulation over time damages relationships. Many adults are manipulative. It's time to address this dangerous area now, in children, before it develops into a lifelong pattern.

Being able to accept no as an answer is a spiritual skill all people need to learn. A lot of temptation is out there, and children need to learn to say no to themselves in order to stay within appropriate boundaries. Salvation provides a framework for us to know what to say no to. Titus 2:11–12 shares these helpful words, "For the grace of God that brings salvation has appeared to all men. It teaches us to say 'No' to ungodliness and worldly passions, and to live self-controlled, upright and godly lives in this present age."

Sometimes as a parent you have to take the difficult road of saying no because you know what damage a yes may do. Furthermore, your hard work now will provide your children with needed character as they get older.

31

Kids need a way to respectfully challenge a parent or another authority. To prepare them to do that in life outside your home, . . .

TEACH KIDS THE WISE APPEAL

THE BIBLE TELLS US THAT GOD GAVE YOUNG DANIEL great wisdom that would someday propel him into leadership in the kingdom wherein he was a captive.

But now, he had a problem. King Nebuchadnezzar required him to eat a diet that wasn't in line with his Jewish convictions. What would he do? Daniel 1:8 says that he "resolved not to defile himself with the royal food and wine." But how on earth would he *keep* that resolution?

Instead of just reacting emotionally and stomping his feet because things weren't going his way, Daniel appealed to the chief official, offering a new idea that persuaded those in authority to adjust their position to accommodate his wishes. Daniel made a *wise appeal,* and it changed the situation. The practical tool of a wise appeal is something that can help children of all ages know how to respond to an authority in a respectful, yet persuasive way.

When children don't get their way, they often react emotionally. Parents must remain firm, not only to avoid a dangerous option for their kids, but also to teach the character quality of contentment, being happy with what they have instead of always wanting more. But there needs to be a way for children to appeal to parents. When kids learn a wise appeal, they're able to use it with authorities both inside and outside the home. The idea comes from the Bible.

The wise appeal is also illustrated in Scripture in the lives of Esther and Nehemiah, who each had to go to an authority to present a difficult situation. Nehemiah talked to the king and proposed a plan. He didn't just complain about his problems or become defiant. He looked for a way to bring about change. His success happened, in part, because of the way he made his request (Nehemiah 2:4–6).

The wise appeal is a godly alternative to whining, badgering, and arguing, but at the same time, it's important that the child also be able to accept a no answer. The wise appeal isn't just another manipulative tool to get parents to change their minds. Sometimes the answer is still no.

When you take the time to teach and practice a wise appeal in family life, you help your children develop a tool they'll use outside the home as well. After all, people young and old regularly find themselves in positions requiring that they appeal to an authority.

Here's what the wise appeal looks like and how you can teach it to your children even as preschoolers, and surely in their teen years. Let's say your child wants to challenge a decision or try to reverse the answer to a request. His or her wise appeal may go something like this: (1) "I understand that you want me to . . ." (2) "I have a problem with that because . . ." (3) "So could I please . . . ?"

Note the three-part approach. The first phrase helps the child identify with the concerns and needs of the parent. When moms and dads feel understood, they're more likely to listen to alternatives, negotiate, or compromise. It's interesting how a respectful beginning to a wise appeal often melts a parent's resistance. When a child expresses the parent's concern in a way that communicates true understanding, that mom or dad feels encouraged.

The second phrase helps the parent understand the child's predicament and reason for discussion. It also helps the child articulate his or her issue, instead of whining about things.

In the third phrase the child offers a creative solution that addresses both the mom or dad's position and the child's concerns.

You may say to your seven-year-old son, "It's time to clean up the playroom now. We have to go run errands." If he's just gotten involved in his train set, he might answer, "I know you want me to clean up because we're going out; I have a problem with that because I just set up my train track. Could I please leave my train out until we get home so I can play with it later?"

As soon as you realize he's invested time in setting up his train set, you may be willing to adjust your instruction. His idea tells you that he's ready to go on errands with you but that he wants to play when he gets back. Leaving his train set out may be a perfectly acceptable alternative. In fact, many wise appeals reveal solutions that are acceptable to parents because they now have more information. One dad said, "I like the wise appeal because sometimes my daughter shares a solution that's better than mine. I'd have suggested it in the first place if I'd thought about it." The wise appeal often brings more information to the table and creates a good compromise.

On the other hand, maybe you know that company is coming over later and you can't have a train track all over the playroom floor, so you must stick to your original plan. A child in this situation needs to be able to take no for an answer. A child who can't accept "no" without throwing a tantrum isn't ready to use the wise appeal and should lose it as a privilege while he practices obedience.

Some children may try to use the wise appeal in a manipulative way or may not be mature enough to handle it. They may even try using it to get out of doing a job altogether. That's unacceptable. The wise appeal results in a contract between parent and child. This contract requires trust, and when a child proves responsible, he or she then earns the privilege of more trust. Sometimes, it's even helpful to write down the conclusion so there's no bickering about what was decided.

Children learn that the wise appeal isn't a magic formula. They don't always get what they want, but many times it does work to bring about a compromise and change an authority's mind. It's just a tool, but a great one in the hands of a person willing to use it wisely.

One boy appealed to his coach to allow him to play third base. The coach kept him in the outfield for the rest of that game but did put him at third base in the next game, partly because of the appeal but also partly because the boy had a good attitude when he didn't get what he wanted right away. He'd learned the wise appeal at home and had practiced it for years.

The wise appeal teaches children that they don't have to be victims in life. Instead they can be instruments for change. Many people don't like the position they're in and resort to complaining. Others look for solutions in life. The wise appeal is one tool that can help kids realize that they have recourse when things don't go their way.

If you want your child to be a world-changer or a problem solver, the home is an excellent place to learn the skills needed and to practice them. A wise appeal teaches children how to compromise, think of others' needs, communicate, and negotiate. Unfortunately, many children don't learn those skills, and view themselves as victims under the control of others. The wise appeal empowers kids to take charge of their own unhappiness and do something about it.

By teaching the wise appeal, you teach children an adult skill they can use forever.

32

It's important to have a plan when you correct kids; otherwise you may not be effective in your approach. One thing that can keep you focused in the right direction is to remember to . . .

USE CORRECTION TO CHALLENGE THE HEART

"I'M CONCERNED ABOUT MY SON, RICHARD," TINA said to her pastor. "Whenever I discipline him, he gets angry and, even when I give him consequences, he doesn't seem to change."

The pastor had seen the problem himself at church. He knew what Tina was talking about. Richard was thirteen; for years he had seemed to resent any form of correction. "It seems to me that your son lacks a repentant heart."

"I agree," said Tina. "But I bring him to church all the time. I don't know what else to do."

"Repentance is a change of heart and comes with time and practice. Let's look at some ways we might adjust your strategy to bring about the heart change that Richard needs." The pastor shared several ideas and strategies that Tina used with her son. Change was slow but consistent, and over time Richard made significant adjustments in the way he responded to correction. Here are some of the things Tina learned.

When people need to change their ways, the Bible uses the term *repentance* to describe the process. (See, for example, Luke 3:8, Acts 20:21, and Romans 2:4.) Yet, using words like *repentance* and *sin* too often in correction with kids may create an unbalanced view of God

128

and his positive plan for life. Whether you use the term *repentance* or not, however, it's good to understand what God has to say about it.

The word *repent* simply means "to change one's mind" and in its various forms is used over one hundred times in the Bible. From these verses we learn that there are six different parts to repentance, and they all have practical implications for parenting.

The first step in repentance, for example, is to settle down, stop fighting, and be willing to work on the problem. Jeremiah 8:6 says that an unrepentant person is like a horse charging into battle. You can visualize the nostrils flared and the steam coming out of the horse's mouth. That picture could easily resemble some children when they're corrected. The solution is that they need to settle down.

Unfortunately, some parents continue on with the correction while the child is still upset. It would be better to require that the child go into the other room or the hall and settle down before continuing the correction process. Parents who take advantage of this first step in repentance slow down the process and decrease the intensity, and thus see more significant change in their kids.

The other steps in repentance include admitting that you've done something wrong (see 1 Kings 8:47), otherwise known as *confession*; acknowledging that there must be a better way (see Matthew 3:8–10); and committing to doing the right thing (see Jeremiah 34:14). Two other steps of repentance involve more emotion. They're feeling sorrow for doing the wrong thing (Jeremiah 31:19), and having a desire to do what's right (Romans 7:14–15). These last two steps involve emotions and desires and are the ultimate goal in the change process. However, just because you don't see the remorse or a desire to do what's right, that shouldn't stop you from pursuing the goal. Some children need correction over a long period of time in order to make the changes necessary in their emotions.

To work through the elements of repentance with Richard, it was often helpful to have a conversation at the end of the discipline time. That *positive conclusion* reviews the offense, discusses why it was wrong, and helps children develop a plan for next time. After all, repentance involves confession. Parents who simply give a consequence and hope that kids are making the connection to their poor thinking are often disappointed with the slow process of change. In a debriefing after an offense, it's valuable for children to admit their part of the problem. Articulating what went wrong is an important step toward change. Sometimes children don't believe they've done anything wrong. Or they think that the other person started it, justifying their response. Of course, children are responsible for their own responses, whether they started it or not. A sarcastic answer or a returned punch can't be excused simply because the other person instigated.

One dad reported success with his son this way: "I used to have a justice mentality. 'You did that, so you deserve this.' I even had a list of consequences on the refrigerator for various offenses. I'd give the consequences, but I rarely saw significant change. It wasn't until I started implementing these steps of repentance that we really began to see change in our son."

After correction, other steps—like restitution, reconciliation, or an apology—are often needed for restoring relationship. To avoid having children say, "I'm sorry" while not feeling it in their hearts, we encourage children to say, "I was wrong for . . . . Will you forgive me?" This statement doesn't require an emotion but is an act of the will. A child should be able to take responsibility for an offense whether it's provoked or not. Of course, if the child truly feels sorrow for the offense, then "I'm sorry" is certainly the way to begin reconciliation.

Be careful about disciplining only one child when two kids are fighting. Both are usually at fault in some way. Trying to figure out who started it rarely leads to peace. Victims are often instigators. Teach children how to respond to offenses, and when they make a mistake, teach them how to admit it and ask for forgiveness.

God our Father and Jesus used positive conclusions in their discipline. Adam and Eve sinned, and although God imposed the consequence of leaving the garden, he took time with them, made clothes out of animal skins, and gave them a hope for the future (Genesis 3:21). After the resurrection Jesus met with Peter and asked him three times, "Do you love me?" Peter needed a positive conclusion after his three denials of Christ. After Peter answered yes, Jesus affirmed Peter's ongoing future with words such as "Feed my lambs" and "Take care of my sheep" (John 21:15–17). When David sinned with Bathsheba, the consequence was that their baby died. Shortly thereafter, Bathsheba got pregnant again, and the same prophet who had foretold their first son's death came to David and said of the new baby, "Name him Jedidiah," which means "loved of the Lord" (2 Samuel 12:24–25). After an offense, our kids need to hear the same kind of message that God gave to Adam and Eve and David and that Jesus gave to Peter: "We've dealt with it. Let's move forward. We have work to do." That positive focus to discipline helps children experience freedom in their consciences, a much-needed gift when they've sinned or made a mistake.

A theology of repentance is a necessary part of a biblical parenting philosophy. It's a powerful way of looking at the correction of children, resulting in deeper, more significant change. Kids need to adjust more than their behavior. They also need to change their hearts. If you embrace these few suggestions, kids are forced through a process. You can't force a change of heart, but you can teach kids a way to think about what they've done wrong, and take them through predictable steps so they'll know what healthy thinking looks like and can process their mistakes in a godly way.

God is the expert at changing the heart, and we must look to him for guidance in this delicate area. Praying regularly for soft hearts on the part of children can go a long way toward helping them be responsive to correction.

33

Considering the controversy around corporal punishment and the desire to maximize change in children, especially during correction, it's important that you decide whether . . .

To Spank or Not to Spank

THE TOPIC OF SPANKING CREATES CONTROVERSY IN many Christian parenting circles today. Although we don't expect to deal with all the issues surrounding this subject, we would like to address the topic and provide you with some thoughts as you develop your own biblical philosophy of parenting.

Two camps appear when it comes to the discussion of spanking. On the one hand, some parents believe that spanking is the silver bullet of parenting. These folks believe that spanking is required if you're going to follow the Bible and raise your child according to God's principles. On the other hand, there are those who believe that spanking is wrong and results in children who are emotionally disturbed and have tendencies toward violence. We disagree with both of these extremes.

First, let's go to the Bible. Those who argue for spanking often turn to the book of Proverbs where it refers to using the *rod* with children five times (13:24, 22:15, 23:13, 23:14, 29:15). Interestingly enough, there are three times the term *rod* is used for disciplining adults (10:13, 14:3, 26:3), but you don't hear people talking much about those verses. Another helpful verse to throw into the discussion that actually suggests that spanking may not be best in some circumstances is Proverbs 17:10: "A rebuke impresses a man of discernment more than a hundred lashes a fool."

More importantly, an honest study of the book of Proverbs reveals over ninety references to correction without the use of spanking. For example, the word *rebuke* is used over ten times, *correct* eight times, *discipline* at least five times, and so on. So what do we conclude that the Bible says about spanking? We might define the *rod* as a general term for correction, but even if it refers to spanking as a physical strike on the bottom of a child, it's clear from Proverbs that it's one tool in the toolbox, but not the only one.

On the other hand, some believe that children who are spanked in childhood become more aggressive, violent, and emotionally challenged. We would suggest that thinking is flawed, because it doesn't consider another factor: parental anger. We do believe that a spanking delivered with parental anger is dangerous and counterproductive in the correction process. In these situations the anger of the parent can be damaging to the child and to the parent/child relationship. A more effective line of thinking would separate the anger and the spanking and look at them as independent factors, resulting in different conclusions about spanking. It's not the spanking that's damaging but the anger often associated with it.

We do find that some situations warrant restraint from spanking. First, if the parent tends to react with anger, it would be better to choose from a host of different choices for consequences and not use spanking. Second, if spanking isn't working. It's interesting to note that spanking doesn't seem to bring about change in some children, for a host of different reasons. Third, if the children aren't your kids. You might laugh at that last reason, but parents who rely on spanking as their primary discipline technique find themselves in a difficult situation when the neighbors are over playing at their house and need to be disciplined. A heart-based strategy for change in a child provides techniques for your own children and for those who happen to need discipline while in your home or classroom.

Many families adopt or work with kids in the foster care program, as I (Scott) did, and often must agree not to spank the child in our care. That's wise given some of the backgrounds of the children in these programs, understanding that child abuse or angry outbursts were often part of the child's former life, creating misunderstanding about spanking.

It's important to remember that the goal of discipline is a changed heart. Sometimes spanking offers a fast and effective tool to bring about heart change. Other times, parents simply use spanking as a behavior modification strategy, thinking they are pleasing God because spanking is in the Bible, but really missing the heart of God because they're simply focusing on behavior and not the heart.

If spanking is to be used, it's most appropriate for young children, recognizing that as kids grow older, parents have more cognitive correction strategies they can use to maximize heart change. Spanking might best be reserved for outright defiance on the part of the child and as a last resort, avoiding the temptation to overuse it. As with any consequence, overuse weakens effectiveness.

Some advise that spanking be done with the hand so that the parent can feel the pain and to avoid abuse. Others believe that a neutral object such as a paddle or wooden spoon is better than using the hand, leaving the hands for loving and affection. These attempts to define spanking and its use are more about personal preferences that parents must determine for themselves. What's important, however, is that any form of correction needs to be done within the context of relationship. After any consequence, be sure to have a debriefing time to demonstrate forgiveness and reconciliation.

Parents must decide whether spanking will be a tool in their correction toolbox. If you decide to use spanking, then you'll want to be controlled and use it strategically, focusing on heart change. There are many families today who have used spanking and many who haven't. In both camps are families who have raised godly children who love the Lord and want to follow him, and who are well-adjusted emotionally. The issue has more to do with the bigger picture of correction and teaching. Discipline is about training and equipping.

Keep in mind that spanking is just a tool. Whether you use it or not depends on a number of factors in your own home that involve your children as well as you as a parent. Focus on the goal of a changed heart, use a multi-faceted approach to help your child change, pray that God will give you wisdom for each day, and he will help you know whether spanking is a helpful tool in your toolbox of consequences.

34

It's a privilege to have coaches, teachers, and other leaders involved in your child's life, but they often have different approaches. Even when they do it differently, be sure to . . .

SUPPORT OTHER AUTHORITIES WHO WORK WITH YOUR KIDS

"I CAN'T BELIEVE THAT COACH IS YELLING AT MY SON. I'm going over there to give him a piece of my mind!" We can all identify with the frustration of that dad who believes his son is being mistreated by an angry coach. But wait. Might a different approach make for more lasting growth in this child?

As children grow older, they have other leaders and authorities influencing their lives. Coaches, teachers, youth leaders, and other caregivers provide children with alternate sources of leadership. Many of those leaders direct children differently than you would. The coach may use a harsher approach, for example. The youth leader may be more relational. But each of those significant people leaves an important impression on your child.

The older a child gets, the more important other leaders become. Children benefit from different styles of leadership. They also learn complementing lessons from others that aid in their development. The challenge is finding leaders who teach your values and beliefs instead of those that might undermine your parenting. You're likely on the lookout for danger signs that your values are being challenged, but sometimes the warning flags go up too soon simply when the relational style is different or when a leader has a more firm, or even harsh, approach.

Consider this example. Colin is fourteen. He's been late to class several times and isn't doing well at turning in his homework. His dad would say, "He's just sloppy. He could do better. He just doesn't seem to care as much as he should."

Then came the missed opportunity. Colin was late to the pre-game baseball practice, so the coach didn't let him start. In fact, he didn't even let him play until the last inning. He told Colin, "I told you that you need to get here on time. You've been late several times. If you want to play, be here on time."

Colin hadn't just been lazy. They had car trouble, so Dad decided to take matters into his own hands. He yelled at the coach for being harsh with his son. Dad made a strategic error in defending his son instead of using it as a teaching opportunity for Colin. After all, had Colin developed a reputation of being on time at every practice, the coach might then have given him the benefit of the doubt. Furthermore, tardiness was a real problem for Colin. Many times Colin was late and justified himself with what he believed was a good reason.

It would have been better to use the lost game time as an opportunity to teach his son the value of being on time and building a good reputation with those in charge. The same truth might then have been applied to school and homework.

Sometimes other leaders and authorities need correction, or they need advice about how to work with your child. However, stop for a moment before you challenge the leadership and undermine the authority of that influence in your child's life. Might you make a more strategic choice to gain a learning experience for your child?

It may be better to talk with the child afterward, perhaps saying, "It seemed like the coach was pretty upset because you weren't on time. What are some ways you can communicate to the coach that you'll work on this and do better next time?"

A biblical parenting philosophy recognizes that other leaders and authorities are strategic in the life of your child, and although they often relate in different ways than you prefer, supporting them can strengthen your work in your child's life. If you step back and look at the situation for a moment, here's what you'll see: your child has a weakness. That weakness was revealed in another setting, and a leader took some disciplinary action, maybe a tougher approach than you would have liked. However, it's discipline nonetheless. You, then, are spared the task of issuing a consequence. It's been done for you. Instead, you get to act as counselor or coach. What a great opportunity to help your child learn, and you don't have to be the bad guy.

Your children need help processing how best to relate to other leaders and authorities in their lives. After all, as your kids grow up they'll likely have bosses that lead differently than you do. Now is an excellent time to teach children how to relate to various kinds of authority, even when a leader is harsh.

Other leaders in a child's life may do it differently, allowing you an opportunity to teach your kids valuable lessons. The flip side of this principle is also true. Sometimes another leader or authority can teach your child something you haven't been able to communicate successfully.

For example, a youth leader may give your son a vision for working hard in school because the good grades will help him get into college. Of course, you've been saying that for years, but your son hasn't listened. Somehow the youth leader made the connection.

Look for ways to get your kids under other people's leadership in order to pass on good values and convictions to them. That's one of the reasons many parents have their children take piano lessons, get involved in church youth group, or join a scouting program.

One mom said, "My son lacked confidence and self-control. So when he expressed an interest in martial arts, I was thrilled. I signed him up right away. The instructors are firm and teach the kids respect and self-control. My son has joined the leadership track now and is gaining more self-confidence, as he has to be in front of the group, leading exercises and activities."

Schoolteachers have to deal with all kinds of parents. Some parents blame the teachers for a child's poor performance. Other parents criticize the teachers for being too hard on the kids. Make sure your child's teachers know that you're grateful for their leadership and that you support them. Furthermore, encourage them to pull your child aside and offer words of advice or correction. When teachers know that you're supportive, they're much more inclined to take initiative and go out of their way to help your child.

When you teach children to value other leaders and authorities, you're teaching them how to apply an important concept from the Bible. First Peter 2:13–14 says, "Submit yourselves for the Lord's sake to every authority instituted among men: whether to the king, as the supreme authority, or to governors, who are sent by him to punish those who do wrong and to commend those who do right."

One quality children need to learn in life is responsiveness to authority. As a parent, you're already trying to teach that to your kids regularly by giving them instructions, holding them accountable, and providing direction. Kids need to learn how to transfer that quality to other leaders and authorities as well. That may not be easy when a teacher leads differently than the child is used to.

Other leaders in a child's life can enhance your work as a parent, so look for ways to support them. Take advantage of the differences to teach your kids about leadership and submission. If children are able, have them try to evaluate different styles of leadership to encourage them to learn from a situation. What makes a good coach or an effective teacher? Likely the answer to that question has to do with leadership gifts.

As you teach children various ways to support leaders in their lives, you're preparing them for many challenges they'll face in the future. Good responses to leadership start now and have significant ramifications for your child's life.

35

Ultimately, it's God who changes a child's heart, so you'll want to know . . .

How to Pray for Your Kids

TIM IS NOW AN ADULT, BUT HE TELLS THE STORY OF the time when he was ten and got caught stealing a small toy from a store. His dad had to come to the store to pick him up and talk to the police. When they got home, Tim had imagined that his dad would yell at him and ground him. Instead, he told his son to go to his room, because as a dad, he needed to spend some time praying. After about a half hour, Tim's dad came into his room and calmly talked to him about stealing, bad friends, and about God. As Tim looks back, he now sees how significant his dad's response was to this crisis in his life. He said, "I always knew my dad was praying for me. That knowledge stayed with me all my years. I think it's one of the greatest gifts my dad gave me."

It's important for parents to be in the habit of regularly praying for their kids. Not only does prayer change your child but it also helps you as a parent align yourself with God and his plan. With his strength you'll be less likely to blow up in anger, and you'll have more wisdom for dealing with life's challenges. Remember that God created your child, so he knows and loves him more than you do. God has called you to parent this child, and he can give you the tools and wisdom you need to do the job.

Each day, pray that God will give you the strength to maintain personal control as you work with your children. One dad said it this way: "I felt so frustrated with my daughter's selfishness that I would often get angry with her. I realized that my response wasn't helping, but rather, was hurting the situation. I decided to start praying for my daughter every morning. It's amazing what God did in my heart. I was able to be firm with her and keep my own emotional intensity under control."

It's tempting to blow up in anger or give in to constant nagging. Parenting requires continual perseverance and strength. God provides spiritual resources when emotional resources seem scarce. Learning to trust in him and pray every day for strength and wisdom will go a long way toward enabling you to face the challenges of parenting.

Also, pray that God will change your child's heart. It's important to note that nowhere in the Bible does it say that parents change children's hearts. We do read that people can change their own hearts. God calls that *repentance*. We also see that God changes people's hearts directly. Ezekiel 36:26 reveals this promise: "I will give you a new heart and put a new spirit in you; I will remove from you your heart of stone and give you a heart of flesh." That's the prayer we want to have for our children every day.

Of course, God does use parents as instruments to motivate kids to change their hearts, so your prayer will be one that allows you to partner directly with God in changing your child's heart.

You'll also want to pray for relational connection opportunities in the course of your day. After all, much of the business of family life requires that you be firm with your children. That toughness often wears at the relationship, so times of connection are important. Remember that children can only take as much pressure as the relationship allows. Ask the Lord to provide some fun times in your day or a meaningful conversation or a moment where you and your child are able to connect in a deeper way. Those moments are precious. They often come at bedtime or when a child needs comfort, or even in the midst of correction. Pray that God will give you those moments in your day to strengthen your relationship together.

Also take time to pray that God will provide you with teaching opportunities. Sometimes it's a thoughtful comment or a creative idea that connects with a child's heart. Teaching opportunities often come spontaneously as gifts directly from the Lord. So, take time to pray for insight and wisdom on how best to parent your child. Pray that God will prepare your heart for the teachable moments and make you sensitive to them. God may use your own walk with him to give you an idea, or you may discover a truth in a book you're reading or some advice you've heard. Be on the lookout for tools for teaching. Just like any good teacher, you want to always be looking for ideas and ways to bring about the lightbulb moments in your children's hearts. God often provides those, so don't hesitate to ask him for them.

"My prayer life sure grew when my son became a teenager!" shared one mom. "I realized how vulnerable he was and how little I could really do about it. I began praying fervently for his safety when he was with friends; I prayed that he would make wise choices and that he would learn to trust the Lord for himself. I even prayed that if he was doing the wrong thing, he'd get caught. I learned to trust God with my son's life and heart, realizing that God loved him more than I did." Raising kids can teach us a lot about trusting God.

The reality is that parenting is the toughest job in the world. We need all the help we can get. God promises us that we can ask him for wisdom and he'll give it to us. James 1:5 says, "If any of you lacks wisdom, he should ask God, who gives generously to all without finding fault, and it will be given to him."

Parenting often brings us to our knees. Sometimes we think we know what we're doing as parents, but that feeling of confidence doesn't usually last too long. In fact, our weakness as parents often gives us a greater appreciation of our heavenly Father, who wisely provides guidance, discipline, and strength in just the right measure for us.

During your prayer time, take a moment and thank God for his faithfulness to you. One of the greatest gifts we have is being part of God's family. We are his children if we have trusted Christ as Savior.

That's an awesome privilege that we enjoy. In fact, you'll want to pray regularly that you can help your children understand God's grace in that same way. As you express to your children the appreciation you have for God's love and mercy in your life, your prayer is that they'll see the need to seek God for themselves and develop a personal relationship with him.

When family life gets difficult and you feel stressed by the challenges of the day, remember to go to the Lord for strength. You may even want to check out the "911 Psalm" in the Bible. Psalm 91:1–2 says, "He who dwells in the shelter of the Most High will rest in the shadow of the Almighty. I will say of the LORD, 'He is my refuge and my fortress, my God, in whom I trust.'" We all need rest and a fortress sometimes. God is our strength. Prayer is the vehicle God designed to transport your heart into his presence. Use it often and you'll be a better parent for it.

36

Children can develop tendencies toward angry responses when they aren't pleased with life situations. It's not wise to ignore the problem, but rather recognize that . . .

A Child's Anger Problem Needs Attention

"Aagh!"

Mom realized what was about to happen and walked closer to the playroom to see what her son was frustrated with now. She entered the door just in time to see the toy go flying across the room. No one else was around. Jake had a problem with anger, and when he got upset, he would lose control, often throwing, hitting, or yelling at whatever was closest. Sound familiar? If so, you'll want to help children view anger as energy and develop a plan to manage it.

The child who gets frustrated with a puzzle or argues with a friend needs to learn how to deal with the energy building inside before exploding. Children can slow things down inside their hearts before the eruption, and you as the parent can teach them to do so. An anger management plan needs several components, and one essential step is to teach kids to stop when their emotions are telling them to push forward.

Anger can motivate children as well as adults to act out and say or do things that they regret afterward. Many children, however, have more emotion than they're able to manage easily. That's why they need an essential heart quality that God calls *self-control*. Proverbs 29:11 says, "A fool gives full vent to his anger, but a wise man keeps himself under control."

Before you move on, be sure to read that verse again. After all, there's a lot of contemporary thinking out there that encourages people to vent or release their anger in order to regain emotional control. That's not what the Bible teaches. Rather, the solution is to develop a biblical philosophy of parenting that views emotions in a positive light while encouraging self-control to keep them in check. Please don't think this means repressing anger or stuffing it down so that it comes out later with a vengeance. Self-control simply means managing the energy that anger provides in a way that is productive. Kids can learn to do this, but it takes training and a lot of God's grace. To help your family develop more anger control, it's best to use a "Stop" technique to slow things down instead of allowing them to escalate.

Ryan is quite emotional. When he doesn't get his way, he reacts with anger. Dad and Mom are using a number of strategies to help their son, but one strategy seemed to have a significant impact. "We talked about anger as energy. We told Ryan that the energy could be used for good or bad, and he needed to pull back instead of push forward in order to figure out how best to use it. He decided that when he got angry, he would either sit down or walk away. It worked, and we encouraged him to continue to use that new strategy."

You may want to use pictures of stop signs to illustrate this for your kids. The size of the stop sign for a child depends on the intensity of the anger. Children who are very upset need a larger stop sign to handle the challenge, but children must learn to handle the small frustrations of life as well. Sometimes a small stop sign is all that's needed, simply taking a deep breath or engaging in another activity or leaving the situation. The child needs to take time to acknowledge that frustration is developing and that anger is present.

With young children, visualizing three different-size stop signs can illustrate your point. The small one is simply taking a few deep breaths. The medium stop sign also may include walking around a bit to allow the emotion to settle. The largest stop sign is a defined break from the situation, and the child needs to sit in another room or away from the situation, with the goal of settling down.

Stopping is helpful whether the child is just becoming frustrated or is already quite angry. This step is especially important for the child who is enraged. Rage is anger that controls you no matter how well you conceal it. The primary way to tell that children are enraged is that they can no longer think rationally and their anger is now controlling them. They've lost control.

The solution to rage is always to stop. When a child is enraged, you might say, "You're too angry to talk about this right now. Go spend some time alone. Come back when you can tell me in a calm voice why you're angry and we'll continue to talk."

Here's the challenge. Children who have an anger problem don't want to stop. They want to push forward, showing their displeasure, determined to get what they want, and sometimes are even manipulative with their anger to control the situation. Stopping doesn't seem natural, and kids, who lack self-control, enter anger episodes of various magnitudes.

Whatever you do, don't jump into the battle with your kids. When they're angry, children look for ways to draw you into a fight. Avoid it. It's not productive and often escalates the problem. Rather, learn how to stop, and teach your kids to do the same. By slowing down the process, you'll gain a greater ability to interact with your kids without the complications that anger interjects. If you choose to fight it out with emotional intensity, then the problem is no longer a heart problem in the child. It's now a conflict management problem between two angry people.

A good anger management plan looks to decrease three things: the intensity of the emotion a child experiences, the frequency of anger episodes, and length of the recovery time. When parents and kids work on an anger plan, children develop more self-control. Here are several guidelines for anger management in a home. Make these a regular part of your routine and you'll see significant progress.

1. Never argue with children who are angry. Have them take a break and continue the conversation later.
2. Identify the anger cues that reveal your child is about to lose control. Point them out early, and stop the interaction. Don't wait for explosions before you intervene.
3. Help children recognize anger in its various disguises, such as a bad attitude, grumbling, glaring, or a harsh tone of voice.
4. Debrief after the child has settled down. Talk about how to handle the situation differently next time. You may even want to practice a better way to handle it.
5. Teach children constructive responses. They could get help, talk about it, or walk away. These kinds of suggestions help children have a plan for what they should do, not just what they shouldn't do.
6. When angry words or actions hurt others, individuals should apologize and seek forgiveness.

By doing these things you'll teach your children to do what Colossians 3:8 says: "Rid yourselves of all such things as these: anger, rage, malice, slander, and filthy language from your lips." It takes work to develop emotional control, and the family is often the laboratory for that growth to take place.

Remember that the child's anger is the child's problem. Miriam was fifteen when she finally got a handle on her anger issues. When you ask her what her secret was, she says, "I think I finally realized that this was my problem. I was used to seeing my anger as everyone else's problem, and if they would change, then I wouldn't be angry. When I came to that realization, it was freeing for me, because then I had more control over the solution."

Anger control is an important skill for children to learn, and there's no better time than now. Implementing a formal stop in response to growing emotion helps children regain control and keeps the problem in perspective.

Many adults don't know how to deal with their increased intensity and push forward instead of backing off. The natural inclination when angry is to become more intense, but the best solution is to lower the intensity before moving forward. Parents who require this kind of process will get much further when helping their children deal with anger.

37

When children don't get what they want, they may complain and make life miserable for those around them. If this is true . . .

TEACH KIDS TO BE SOLVERS INSTEAD OF WHINERS

JOHNNY IS A WHINER. HE COMES INTO THE KITCHEN and says to Mom, "Moooom, I'm hungry," with that whiny voice that sounds like fingernails on a chalkboard. Every time she turns around, Mom hears Johnny's whining. What's a mother to do? The problem is bigger than just the whiny voice. It's a way of looking at life and problems. Working on whining in a child's life is an important part of your biblical philosophy of parenting because it's helping children face problems from a godly perspective.

Problems make great opportunities to teach children to face life's challenges. There are two kinds of people in the world: solvers and whiners. Whiners complain about life, feel like victims, and believe that others cause their problems. If others would just change, then they'd be happy. Until then, they'll just whine about life.

Solvers, on the other hand, look for solutions, recognize that they can impact others, and feel empowered to change life. If they can't solve the problem themselves, they know where to go to get solutions.

Helping children move from being whiners to being solvers starts in the way they talk about problems or bring them to their parents. The very words they use are important. When Johnny comes into the kitchen and says, "I'm hungry," try saying, "Johnny, that's focusing on the problem. Tell me the solution."

Johnny's response can be, "Mom, could I please have a snack?" That's using words to focus on the solution. Don't wait for the whiny voice to indicate a complaining heart. Look for word cues and you'll be able to bring about change more quickly and effectively.

When Lori yells, "I can't find my boots!" that's focusing on the problem. It would be better for her to say, "Dad, would you please help me find my boots?"

Maybe you think this is only semantics. But the words children use to bring problems to their parents can mean all the difference in the way they view themselves and the world. Whining is often the sign of a victim mentality. Children who believe they're victims are often angry and resentful because everyone else is the cause of their problems. They don't believe they can change anything, so they may as well just complain about it.

Expressing misery to others may bring sympathy, but it rarely brings change. Furthermore, if the whining works and change occurs, it further cements the wrong thinking in the child's mind. "If I whine enough, other people will change the situation, and then I'll feel better."

Be careful that you don't solve a whining child's problem too quickly. Rather, encourage him or her to take initiative to solve it. The solution may involve you, but it requires that the child take action toward the solution as well.

Twelve-year-old Elizabeth often complains that she doesn't have the clothes she wants to wear. Mom is in the habit of helping her find something, but most of the time Elizabeth is still unhappy about the choice. Mom realized that her daughter had developed an attitude that the clothes problem was Mom's to solve, so she decided to make some changes.

Mom took Elizabeth out clothes shopping, and they bought a couple new outfits. Then she helped Elizabeth organize her closet and drawers, removing many of the clothes she'd outgrown or didn't like. Next, Mom showed Elizabeth how to run the washing machine and helped her with the first few loads. Mom explained to Elizabeth that now she was twelve years old and could manage her own clothes by herself. Mom also took a stand against Elizabeth's complaining.

With these steps Mom empowered her daughter to be a solver when it came to her clothes. Now Elizabeth couldn't blame anyone else for a lack of clean clothes. When she did, Mom told her that she couldn't play on the computer or go out to play with her friends until she washed her clothes. It worked. Elizabeth was still unhappy sometimes with her options for clothes, but she knew that she was the one who could fix it.

Some parents have a low tolerance for frustration, especially when they see that tension in their children. Such parents, in an attempt to ease the pain, step in and rescue the child. Remember that frustration can be a great teacher and provides internal motivation to find a solution. When parents solve too many problems, children come to rely on parental solutions because it's the easy way out. When moms and dads require kids to do the hard work to solve their own problems, the kids develop a greater confidence to handle the challenges of life.

Brian's son Sammy often wanted a drink of juice from the refrigerator. Since Sammy was only four, Brian didn't feel his son could solve that problem by himself. Unfortunately, Sammy whined often for a drink. Brian got an idea. He bought a small pitcher with a lid that held a couple of cups of juice. He then taught Sammy how to use the dishwasher door as a table and pour his own juice into his plastic cup. Any spills weren't a problem because when Sammy was done, he just shut the dishwasher and put the pitcher back in the refrigerator. Brian had empowered his son to be a solver instead of a whiner.

Philippians 2:14 talks about having a good attitude with tasks when it says, "Do everything without complaining or arguing." That's great advice for the family. The fun thing about children who are problem solvers is that they look for ways to help others who have problems. Max, at age nine, used to do a lot of complaining, but after significant work in this area, his parents saw major changes. The real reward for them was when Max had a friend over who was whining. Max looked at him and said, "Why are you whining so much? Why don't you do something about it?"

Mom smiled as she listened to her son. She'd forgotten how much he used to complain. It was encouraging to hear Max have a different outlook on life that even affected others. Parents can empower their children to take responsibility for change and thus be a blessing. It takes some retraining and a lot of work to help kids gain a new perspective about life's challenges, but it's worth it in the end.

38

For kids to have the motivation to do a
thorough or complete job . . .

CHILDREN NEED TO LEARN
HOW TO WORK HARD

ONE MOM TOLD US THIS STORY: "I WENT INTO THE family room, where my children were watching TV, and said in a cheerful voice, 'Hey kids. It's Saturday morning, and we have some work to do before we play today.' You'd have thought that someone announced the end of the world! The idea of work was met with moans and groans and all kinds of negativity. Why can't my kids do a little work without complaining every step of the way?"

If that sounds familiar, you may need to start by changing what your kids believe. Most children believe that their job description in life is to have fun. Parental instructions are an interruption to their lives, chores are an inconvenience, and work is to be avoided as much as possible. Parents often contribute to this thinking error by requiring little of their kids and encouraging them to play and have fun. In fact, have you ever noticed that some parents say to their kids as they go out the door, "Have fun"? Why do they say that? Is having fun the supreme goal of childhood? Furthermore, many of those same parents evaluate a child's day by asking, "Did you have fun?" It's no wonder kids believe that's their mission in life.

The problem with that kind of thinking is that kids then resist anything that looks like work. Having fun is certainly a benefit for both children and adults, but kids also need to learn to work hard in life. Some parents have a parenting philosophy that hesitates to impose work on their children lest they rob them of their childhood or hinder their emotional growth by making them unhappy.

Work, though, has many benefits, and kids should learn how to balance work and play at a young age. Work teaches children skills, provides them with a sense of accomplishment, and encourages character qualities such as initiative, perseverance, and responsiveness to authority.

Children who don't know how to work hard develop a number of character weaknesses. Danny, age eleven, is demanding, always expecting his mother to serve him. Marissa, age six, is lazy and tries to get out of the simplest tasks in life. In fact, her dad says that she spends more energy thinking about how to get out of work than it would require to do the work in the first place.

Connie is sixteen and has a problem with lying. Dad and Mom had tried many things to help their daughter become more honest. After coming to one of our seminars, they realized that one of Connie's problems was she didn't know how to work hard.

Lying is always a shortcut. It's a fast way to avoid punishment, an easy way to look good, or a quick way to excuse a job done partway. Children who have a problem with lying need a multifaceted approach for developing honesty and integrity, and one of the components is learning how to work hard.

When people ignore the "Keep off the Grass" sign and cut across the lawn, they give up their integrity in order to get to their destination more quickly. Instead of taking the longer way around on the sidewalk, such a person values his agenda more than the grass, so he doesn't mind trampling on it. The same thing is true with lying. The child who lies values her own desires so much that she tramples on her own conscience.

The book of Proverbs talks about the value of hard work. Proverbs 14:23 says, "All hard work brings a profit, but mere talk leads only to poverty." Also, Proverbs 6:6 says, "Go to the ant, you sluggard; consider its ways and be wise!"

Hard work builds character. Although it may be easier for you to do the work around the house, it's good training for children to take part in chores. This often requires extra parental energy to assign, manage, and check up on kids, but that effort you do as a parent can translate into small bits of character in a child.

Young children can empty the dishwasher, pick up around the house, vacuum, and help fold clothes. Elementary-age children can set the table, wash dishes, clean bathrooms, and wash floors. Older children can handle more responsibility, like mowing grass, making a meal, or caring for a younger child.

One dad told the story of wanting his thirteen-year-old daughter to learn how to work hard. When she asked for horseback riding lessons, he said, "I'm sorry. We can't afford horseback riding lessons, but I could do an exchange with you if you'd like. I want to rebuild our sidewalk around the house, and I need the concrete broken up with a sledgehammer and hauled into a pile, the dirt dug out, and forms built. If you're willing to do that, so I don't have to pay someone else to do it, I'll pay for horseback riding lessons this summer."

"Oh, I'll do anything if I could have horseback riding lessons!" the girl enthused. So they started to work.

At one point she complained because it was too hot. Dad said, "We're the Carlson family. We work even when it's hot. Come on; I'll go out and work with you." So, Dad worked with her in the hot sun.

Another day she said, "But, Dad, it's raining." Dad said, "We're the Carlson family. We can even work in the rain. Come on; I'll work with you." So they worked together in the rain.

Dad was trying to teach his daughter an important lesson: that hard work overcomes obstacles and doesn't look for excuses. He also wanted her to see that hard work pays off. His daughter enjoyed her horseback riding lessons that summer, but more important, she began to believe that she could work hard and complete a difficult task.

After years of training Dad reported that his daughter was proud of her ability to work hard. Many of her friends gave up quickly, or wouldn't even start a difficult task, but his daughter knew she could work hard and that hard work often got her more than others would get who didn't have the same ability to persevere.

39

Kids often compete with each other and compare themselves to each other, so they need the clear message that . . .

Fair Doesn't Mean Equal

"That's not fair!"

"What about him!?"

These words are common in families with more than one child. Competition comes from comparison and often creates tension in relationships between brothers and sisters as they try to put each other down in order to be first or best.

Comparison between siblings often stems from a faulty belief that fair means equal. "If my little brother gets a privilege, then I should get one too." Or, "When I was younger, you were much harder on me than you are with my little sister." Kids need to learn an important fact about life, and parents usually have opportunities to teach it. Fair doesn't mean equal. In fact, equality often becomes the enemy of fairness.

Fairness treats all kids according to their individual needs, which usually aren't equal. Each child needs different things from parents in order to feel loved and to grow to maturity. Children have different strengths and weaknesses. Focus on your children as individuals, and give to them according to their needs.

Sometimes parents contribute to the competition and comparison in their children by trying to treat their children equally. If William gets new shoes, we buy shoes for his sister too. If she gets new markers, then we buy some for William as well. Children quickly get the idea and use the inequities of life to try to get what they want. An important characteristic of a good biblical parenting philosophy is the ability to minimize competition and comparison by treating children uniquely instead of equally.

It doesn't take long to realize that you can't reasonably treat your children the same. You must treat them differently because they have unique needs, personalities, and strengths. A younger child may stay up later than an older brother because she's still taking naps and doesn't need to go to bed as early as he does. That's not unfair. It's treating children according to their needs.

When children compare themselves to each other, they say they want equality, but that's not really true. What each child really wants is to feel special. When you treat them uniquely, and focus on each child independently, you'll be surprised how much the comparison and competition decreases in your family.

In fact, if you have trouble with comparison and competition with your children, you may want to emphasize their individuality. Intentionally give them different privileges, assignments, and responsibilities. Avoid grouping the children by saying things like, "Kids, it's time to eat," or "Boys, let's get in the car." Instead, use each person's name and give separate instructions. "Tori, please wash your hands and come to dinner." "Andre, please help me finish setting the table."

Teach your children that you don't even try to treat them the same. If a brother sees his sister receiving a reward, and he wants one, too, you could say, "Your sister is working on something in her life, and the reward is for her progress and effort. If you want to work on a character quality in your life, let me know, and I'll think of a reward for you too."

After all, God doesn't treat us all the same. That truth is taught in the story of the talents in Matthew 25:14–30. One man received five, another two, and another one. There's no room for comparison. That's God's choice, and he knows us better than we know ourselves. So, he gives us exactly what we need. The same is true with spiritual gifts. He gives each person a different one. He loves us, and, because of that, he treats us uniquely.

John 21:15–23 contains a fascinating story about the disciples that has application to sibling conflict. Jesus is telling Peter how Peter is going to die. Peter turns and looks at another disciple and says, "What about him?" Jesus answers, "What is that to you? You follow me." In essence Jesus was saying, "I treat each person uniquely. You worry about yourself." What a great lesson to apply to our families. Treat children uniquely instead of trying to treat them all equally.

Another thinking error that has to do with comparison is evident when a child makes the statement, "Everyone's doing it," to manipulate you to give in to a request. This is actually saying, "If all my friends are able to do something, it would be unfair for me not to be able to do it." Kids need to learn that other families live life differently than yours does. Here are some thoughts you can share with your child in these moments.

First, sometimes kids believe that appropriate behavior is determined by the culture. Rather, the rules you set up are based on the values you hold. Different families have different values, so as parents, we need to decide what values and convictions we're going to use to determine the rules and expectations for our own families.

Second, *not* everyone else is doing it. There are many families that set guidelines similar to or even more strict than yours. Children have a tendency to find more permissive families to compare themselves to, so they can ask for more.

Third, recognize that this assertion is a manipulative technique. It makes you feel that you're depriving your kids of something. Parenting is hard work, and too many parents are unwilling to take a stand for what's right and for values that are wholesome and healthy.

Don't let your children manipulate you with, "That's not fair." Instead, use the opportunity to teach them that you're making decisions for each person individually based on what you believe to be best.

40

One of the most important lessons children can learn in life is that . . .

CORRECTION IS VALUABLE

"OF ALL MY JOBS AS A PARENT, THE ONE I FIND THE hardest is correction. Furthermore, it doesn't seem to be that productive. It's not that I don't correct. I have to correct my kids several times a day. The problem is that they always give me a hard time. I know that sounds like an exaggeration, but it's true. They don't like it any more than I do. I wish there was a way to parent without correcting kids." That mom's honesty resonates with many of us.

Correcting children can be exasperating. Part of the problem happens when children respond poorly. They don't appreciate your suggestions or advice. Instead they become defensive, offer excuses, blame others, or even blame themselves. This resistance causes children to miss the benefits of correction. Of course, it's not just a kid problem. Many adults respond poorly when a mate offers some helpful criticism or a boss requires change.

Because correction is a regular part of your work with children, it's important to develop some good ways to think about it as you develop your biblical parenting philosophy. Correction has a number of benefits. Some people have to learn painful lessons through experience before they'll change, while others respond quite well to a rebuke or critique. Correction is one of the tools for learning in life. You may want to engage your kids in a helpful dialogue by asking the question, "How many different ways can you list that people learn?"

For example, from a teacher or from a book. Allow them to list as many as they're able, and then say, "I can think of one you haven't thought of." Then reveal your answer. "People learn things through correction." The sooner a child can appreciate correction, the faster that child will mature.

One fun activity you can do with your children to illustrate the value of correction is to come into the kitchen with a three-foot piece of toilet paper hanging from the back of your shirt collar. It won't take long for your child to notice and make a comment. React defensively by saying something like, "Why do you always pick on me? I don't need to be criticized. There's nothing wrong with the way I'm dressed."

You'll provoke curiosity by walking close by or swinging around. When your child pursues you to grab the toilet paper, run away, saying something like, "I didn't do anything wrong. It's not my fault. People are always picking on me and blaming me for everything."

Of course, when it's all over, take time to talk about how important correction is in life. In fact, you might read Proverbs 12:1: "Whoever loves discipline loves knowledge, but he who hates correction is stupid." (We don't use the word *stupid* in our home, but it's interesting that Solomon used it in this verse.) Does that verse say that the person who is corrected is stupid? No. It says that the person who hates correction is stupid. Why do you think it says that? Maybe it means that the person who doesn't want to be corrected will look stupid because he keeps doing the wrong thing without changing.

Children need a vision for the benefits of correction. Talk to your kids about things you've learned when others have corrected you. Invite your children to correct you in a particular area of your life you're working on. (Of course, they need to learn how to give advice or point out a problem in a gracious way.) Explain how people miss out on the benefits of correction because of a poor response to it. Explore with children the reasons why people don't like to be corrected. These discussions can open the door for children to rethink their own responses.

Heeding correction helps a person become wise. It's better to avoid a trap through correction than to fall into it and have to learn from experience. In fact, many of the valuable lessons of life are learned through correction in one form or another. Although children may not appreciate it, the correction they receive from you is a gift, and your persistence can provide them with the wisdom they need both now and for the future.

Jennifer is a mother of two very different children. Luke is ten, and Jonathan is eight. Luke often has to learn the hard way, while Jonathan is more responsive to correction. "I have to approach my kids in different ways. With Jonathan I can do a little explaining and he's likely to respond well to that. With Luke, it's more of a challenge. I have to set firmer limits and give consequences. Some lessons I don't want him to have to learn from life while I sit idly by, so my consequences become the roadblocks and life experience for him. It's hard because he resists me, but I know that he needs discipline or he'd be in big trouble."

Of course, parents must also recognize the value of correction in order to have the perseverance to hang in there in spite of resistance. Too often parents view correction as an interruption to their lives. They have their agenda and goals for the day. Correction blocks those goals and delays the agenda. But think about it for a moment. It may be that the most important things you say to your child today will come during a correction time.

Be sure to leave margin in your life for correction times so you won't be unduly pressured. But more important, recognize that correction is a valuable tool for teaching children about life. It may be difficult at times, but the hard work will be worth it in the end. Proverbs 6:23 says, "The corrections of discipline are the way to life." The word "life" in that passage is referring to a quality of life. The point is that the person who values correction and learns from it will benefit greatly. Correction is an important part of parenting. Although it can be frustrating to correct a resistant child, it's part of your job.

When children are wrong and need correction, they often must undergo a process of internal acceptance of the wrong and a willingness to move in a new direction. That's heart work. If you're firm against their resistance, children are forced to rethink their ways and readjust their thinking. Be firm and willing to correct a resistant child over and over again to help that child move to another way of responding.

Correction often needs time and persistence to be effective. Rarely do children learn a lesson with one episode. Most need many passes over the same truth in order to catch the importance of change.

41

To make spiritual training interesting and communicate to children that the Bible is relevant and exciting for their lives now, look for ways to . . .

USE CREATIVITY TO TEACH YOUR KIDS SPIRITUAL TRUTHS

"DAD, WHEN ARE WE GOING TO DO ANOTHER ONE OF those fun devotions from the Bible?" Wouldn't you love to hear your kids ask that question? It's not only possible but it's likely when you teach spiritual truths in fun ways. No matter how long you've been a believer, you can teach your children tremendous spiritual lessons. The key is to first be growing spiritually yourself and then passing truths on to your kids.

Deuteronomy 6:6–9 gives these instructions: "These commandments that I give you today are to be upon your hearts. Impress them on your children. Talk about them when you sit at home and when you walk along the road, when you lie down and when you get up. Tie them as symbols on your hands and bind them on your foreheads. Write them on the doorframes of your houses and on your gates."

Notice that the first job of all parents is to nurture their own relationship with God and to cherish the principles of God's Word in their own hearts. Parenting has a way of motivating a person toward prayer and Bible study. It's not too long before any parent realizes that help is needed for raising a child. God is the one who changes a child's heart, and parents are just the vehicles God uses in the process. Parents can partner with the God of the universe to bring about heart change.

Some parents make the mistake of delegating the spiritual training of children to the church, believing that they're doing their spiritual duty by taking their kids to Sunday school and youth group. The church is a great support, but it can't take the place of the home when it comes to passing on a spiritual heritage. Even if you've chosen to send your children to a Christian school, you're still their primary spiritual trainer.

Your transparency at home will do a lot to help open spiritual windows for your child. Take time to pray with your kids about the challenges they face, and thank the Lord for his answers to prayer. You might say, "Son, I'm not feeling well today. Would you please pray for me before I go to work?" Or, "I'll be praying for you and your test today. I'll be eager to hear how it goes." Some parents only pray with their kids before meals or at bedtime, but you want your kids to know that God is available all the time. Prayer makes that truth a reality.

Be creative in teaching kids the value of their spiritual growth. You may keep a growth chart on the back of a door to measure a child's physical growth. Right next to it, jot down milestones of spiritual growth and development, like a child's first communion, his or her baptism, and when that child took an opportunity to share the faith or enjoyed an answer to prayer.

Informal discussions about God provide children with in-life opportunities to see how faith applies to experience. As children see you talking about the Lord during daily activity, they'll recognize the relevance of their spiritual lives. Also take time to set up some kind of formal spiritual training, but be sure to make it fun. The best devotions in family life don't usually happen around a table. With young children you might tell a Bible story in the closet with a flashlight. With an older child you could use a science experiment or cooking exercise to illustrate a spiritual truth.

One dad said, "We boiled three objects—a carrot, an egg, and some coffee beans—and talked about the heat in our own lives and what it does to us. Some people are like the carrot and become more limp and weak with pressure. Some are like the egg and become more hardened to life. And some are like the coffee beans that use the heat to influence their world with a pleasant smell and a nice drink." They laughed together as they talked around the stove, and Dad gave several examples of people he knew who were like the coffee beans and were pleasant to be around.

Next Dad used the story of Joseph in Genesis to talk about the benefits of trials and suffering. Joseph was mistreated by his brothers, sold into slavery, falsely accused by Potiphar's wife, and thrown into prison, but he kept trusting God. He was able to respond well in the midst of difficult problems that came into his life.

Dad reported that the activity was fun for their family, but he continued, "A couple of days later, my son came home from school and said, 'I was like the coffee, Dad.' I didn't know what he meant at first, but he went on to tell me that there was a problem at school that he handled well and remembered the coffee beans we'd boiled."

Even if your mate isn't working with you on the spiritual training of the children, do it faithfully, and you'll see great rewards. One mom said, "I used to be discouraged because my husband wouldn't lead a devotion time in our family. I had to get over that because I knew my kids needed spiritual training and I could give it to them. The amazing thing was that as I began teaching spiritual truths to my kids, my husband became more interested as well. It wasn't long before he was also leading spiritually with the kids."

Creativity can be a challenge sometimes. The most important thing is that you're transparent with your kids. If you are growing spiritually and sharing your growth with your children, it'll make an impact on their hearts. Don't minimize the importance of spiritual training. Sometimes sports, academics, and extra activities crowd out the most important things in a child's life. Remember that teaching spiritual truths to children isn't optional. It's part of our God-given responsibility. Many parents work hard to leave a financial inheritance for their kids. Don't forget to also leave a spiritual heritage for them by passing on the faith.

42

Disagreements, problems, and frustration often set the stage for unhelpful interaction between parents and kids. When that happens, don't push forward in a fight. Rather . . .

WHEN THINGS GET INTENSE, REQUIRE A BREAK

"ONE OF THE MOST HELPFUL TOOLS WE'VE LEARNED from the National Center for Biblical Parenting is the idea of the *break*." That's a comment we've heard over and over again. It may be hard for your kids to grasp at first, but the work of parenting is eased greatly when the break is a routine that's used in your home.

When the intensity increases and your child loses control, it's important to take a break. With small children, as young as two or three years old, have them sit in a particular place, a chair, a carpet square, the hallway, or a bottom step. For older children, send them to the hall, the parent's room, or to another quiet place.

Of course, sending a child to take a break is often met with resistance, especially when a child is angry. That's all the more reason why it's an essential skill to learn. Children must learn to settle down.

Unfortunately, parents often ramp up the intensity with their own emotion when a child gets upset. This leads to an escalation of words and a power struggle. Now the focus is taken off the settling down of a child's heart and instead is placed on the power struggle with the parent.

A break can often be a good step in a correction strategy to force the child to settle down and be ready for the subsequent debriefing about the offense. Taking a break is much better than what's typically referred to as "time-out." The instructions given are simple and clear. "You need to go take a break, change your heart, and come back and see me when you're ready to talk about this." Two differences are important. First, the child knows that the objective in taking a break is a changed heart, and, second, the child helps determine the length of time spent in the break place, coming back only when ready for a debriefing.

These two differences between time-out and a break change the posture of the parent. With time-out, Mom or Dad is the police officer, keeping the child in the chair until the sentence for misbehavior has been served. With a break, the parent is eagerly waiting for the child to return so that positive family life can continue.

Sometimes a child's stubbornness or defiance is obvious. In those moments, stop dealing with the issue at hand and talk about the process of how you're relating. "I can tell you're upset, and it's not good for us to continue until you settle down. You need to take a break and come back when you're ready to continue talking about this calmly." Have the child sit in the hall or on the top step or some other boring place. After the child has settled down, then he or she needs to come back to you and talk about the problem.

If your child comes back without having a heart change, then send the child back again. One dad told the story of seven-year-old Belinda, who was yelling at her brother. "I called her upstairs to talk to me about it, and she began yelling at me. I told her that was inappropriate and to take a break in the hall and settle down. About a minute later she came back but was obviously not changed. Her head was tilted down, her posture was slumping, and her bottom lip was sticking out. I didn't even have to talk with her. I just told her what I saw. 'Belinda, I can tell you're not ready yet. The way you're standing and the expression on your face all tell me that you still have a problem in your heart. I want you to go back until you're ready to come out with a changed heart.'

"This time she stayed away for about twenty minutes, and when she returned, she was obviously different. In fact, I took her head in my hands and looked deep into her eyes and said, 'I can see your heart in there. It looks pretty nice right now. It looks like you're ready to talk about this.' Belinda giggled, and then we continued to talk about the problem. I explained to her that she could not yell at her dad. That was disrespectful even if she's angry. We also talked about the right responses she could have if she was angry with her brother."

That dad used a break to help his daughter settle down and thus maximized the correction process. A break helps parents address heart issues with children and can become a primary discipline technique. It actually comes from the Bible in the teaching of discipline in God's family, the church (Matthew 18; 1 Corinthians 5; 2 Corinthians 2). The idea is basically this: if you can't abide by the principles that make this family work, then you can't enjoy the benefits of family life. The two go hand in hand.

Most children resist the break, especially at first. After all, not many people naturally want to pull back and settle down when they feel angry. That's all the more reason to put a break into practice in your home. It teaches children important self-discipline strategies for their hearts. Over time, they'll learn that pushing forward is the wrong response and usually leads to something they'll regret.

The story of Jonah is a beautiful picture of repentance. Jonah 1:1–2 says, "The word of the LORD came to Jonah son of Amittai: 'Go to the great city of Nineveh and preach against it.'" But Jonah refused, so God had to put him in a break, sitting in the belly of a fish, until he came to a point of repentance in his life. But Jonah 3:1–2 is a beautiful passage. "Then the word of the LORD came to Jonah a second time: 'Go to the great city of Nineveh and proclaim to it the message I give you.'" God gives second chances, but often the person needs a period of repentance in between those opportunities.

If a child refuses to take a break, you have several options depending on the age. With younger children you may physically put them there to help them learn what the break is all about. With older children you might refuse to move forward in family life with any benefits until the child takes a break. Kids need to learn that the break isn't an elective. It's a required course.

The break is an important part of a biblical parenting philosophy, not just a childhood solution. Many parents would benefit from taking a break. One mom said, "I feel a lot of intensity and tend to react without thinking. It's as if my emotions have the ability to bypass my brain. I'm learning to step back and settle down before reacting to my kids. It takes work to understand what's actually going on. I'm learning to slow down and think more about what I'm feeling. I'm making progress, and I'm gaining some insight into how I relate to my kids. They're seeing some changes in me too. I'm becoming less afraid of emotions and more eager to understand them and make the most of them in our family."

If you're struggling with emotional intensity in yourself or your children, then every time you see it rising, slow things down, take a break, and resist the temptation to turn up the heat. That's the first step toward managing conflict in a healthy way.

Don't allow conflict to escalate into a battle. Stop the intensity with a break. It will not only help you stay calm but it will help your children develop some maturity in dealing with their emotions and with conflict.

43

Sometimes children develop the habits of defending, rationalizing, and justifying themselves instead of taking responsibility for offenses. Kids need to learn that . . .

CHILDREN WHO PLAY THE BLAME GAME LOSE

"IT'S NOT MY FAULT. HE STARTED IT."

"I did not. You did."

Isn't it amazing that some children seem to be able to see every factor that went into their current problem except their own part in it? Indeed, some kids have a problem blaming others and not taking responsibility for their part of the problem. In the child's mind, it's always someone else's fault. These children have the ability to see all kinds of reasons why an offense occurs, but can't see how their own actions contributed to it, or at least they don't want to admit it.

When children excuse themselves by blaming others, they miss the point of correction and justify their poor responses. Underlying their thinking is often a misbelief that correction means they're inadequate, unworthy, or even stupid. This misunderstanding of correction often hinders significant progress. After all, one of the ways we learn something is through correction.

Admitting your fault in a given situation isn't optional. In fact, taking responsibility for your part of the problem is the first step toward change. Your job as a parent is to help your child move through a process of confession in a gracious way. Clearly ask a child, "What did you do wrong?" Ask in a gentle way, not accusing. This allows your child to admit what he or she did wrong. Confession is part of a biblical process of repentance. Children must take responsibility for their part of the problem in order to change.

Unfortunately, many parents encourage their children to defend themselves or blame others because of the way they approach the confrontation. When you enter a room and ask the question, "What happened here?" or "Who started it?" you're encouraging kids to rationalize, justify, blame, or defend their actions. When you ask, "Who started it?" do you ever have a child say, "It was me." No. Instead they tend to blame.

It's much more effective to have children evaluate their own part of the problem. Even if a child views himself as a victim, his response to that situation is still important. Kids who lash out because they believe they're right often justify unwise responses to conflict. Your job is to help your kids see that their responses are important whether they were provoked or not.

Of course, some children won't want to admit what they did wrong. In that case it's best to have them sit down somewhere for a while until they're ready. Taking responsibility isn't optional. If a child has forgotten what the offense was, then you can tell him, but don't have him just agree. Ask the question again. It's important for children to admit what they did wrong, and verbally confessing it is part of the process.

The reality is that in most situations, multiple factors contribute to the conflict. Children have an ability to focus on all the other factors except their own. If others were involved, as they often are, a child should not excuse misbehavior by blaming someone else. The foolishness of others doesn't justify a wrong response. All children need to take responsibility for their part of the problem.

A common mistake parents make is to engage in dialogue about the whole situation, trying to figure out who else was wrong, what was fair, or why such things happen. Those questions may be helpful at times, but you'll get much further in helping your children change their hearts if you start by asking, "What did you do wrong?" Your simple question can help children see their own mistakes and learn to take responsibility for them. When two children are fighting, for example, be careful not to focus on just one child's offense or who started it. Usually when two children are fighting, you have two selfish children. Ask each of them this simple question: "What did you do wrong?" Teach the offended child how to respond properly.

Confession is a spiritual skill and is established as God's first step toward change. James 5:16 says, "Therefore confess your sins to each other and pray for each other so that you may be healed." God, of course, requires confession in order for us to receive forgiveness. First John 1:9 says, "If we confess our sins, he is faithful and just and will forgive us our sins and purify us from all unrighteousness." People who confess are empowered to change. Confession does something to a person. It somehow makes his or her offense more obvious. Kids have a way of justifying themselves or rationalizing because someone else did something. Although that may be true, confession helps children see that they had a part in the problem as well. Confession is God's idea and a necessary part of the change process.

Those who blame others continually view themselves as victims, always focusing on others' responsibility. In fact, the blamer believes that his happiness is determined by others' actions. This victim mentality leaves a person feeling helpless, continually complaining about life's problems. A person who takes responsibility for his part of an offense is empowered to change because he recognizes his contribution to the problem.

Refusing to allow blaming and requiring children to take personal responsibility prepares a child to think rightly about offenses. Instead of beating oneself up by saying, "I'm such an idiot" or "I'm never going to get this right," it would be better to simply admit fault, learn from it, and go on.

Lasting change takes place in the heart. Sometimes a child becomes self-protective and lacks the humility necessary for change to take place. Having a simple routine in place for processing offenses can go a long way toward developing right thinking about mistakes. All this can start with a great introductory question, "What did you do wrong?"

44

Some children have a hard time completing a task and staying on track when given an instruction. To help them develop a greater sense of responsibility . . .

HAVE KIDS REPORT BACK

HEATHER WAS FRUSTRATED. "WHEN I TELL MY FIVE-year-old son, Jaden, to get his shoes on because we have to go out, he doesn't come back. When I go looking, I find him sitting on the floor, playing with his cars. And it's not just his shoes. Whenever I tell him to do something, he gets sidetracked. I have to yell at him continually to get anything done."

"I have the same problem with my teenager," reported Samantha. "I tell Sara to finish the dishes and clean up the kitchen, but after she heads to her room, I find the job was only half done."

One way to teach children responsibility in the everyday work of family life is to have them report back after completing a task. Many parents give assignments, assuming that their kids are completing the jobs, often resulting in frustration when they later find out that the jobs weren't done, or were only done partway.

Both these moms need to use their frustration to identify the cause of the problem. Kids may be easily distracted, but the deeper issue has to do with irresponsibility. When children are taught to report back, they learn responsibility.

Most children don't naturally feel an internal weight of responsibility. You can help develop it by requiring them to report back. Heather may say, "Jaden, you need to get your shoes and bring them back to me now. I'm going to wait right here in the doorway for you to report back."

As Heather waits, she watches for distraction. At first, Jaden may need very close monitoring, but as he realizes that he needs to report back and that Mom hasn't forgotten about the job, he'll feel the pressure to accomplish the task. Children who do a job partway, easily get distracted, or don't complete tasks need closer supervision, smaller tasks, and more frequent times of checking in.

Even older children sometimes have a problem with irresponsibility. Yelling isn't necessary—more accountability is. It takes work to require kids to report back, but your investment now will give your children a valuable gift. Reporting back after completing an assignment is an adult skill. Employers appreciate it when employees report back. Whether children are three, eight, twelve, or fifteen, they need to learn this valuable skill.

Responsibility can be defined in different ways for different children. For the child who is easily distracted, responsibility could be defined as "sticking to a task until it's completed and you report back." For a child who tends to do a halfhearted job, you might define responsibility as "doing a job thoroughly without being reminded." For the child who tends to do what you said and not what you meant, you might say, "Responsibility is completing the job up to the expectations of the person giving the instruction." In each case you're teaching children what it means to do a job with a sense of obligation to complete it well.

When receiving an instruction, the child should feel a little uncomfortable. That uncomfortable feeling is what responsible people feel when they have an unfinished assignment. Just imagine your own to-do list. If the time is ticking away and your to-do list isn't getting smaller, you feel a bit uncomfortable and put in more effort. Children often don't feel that uncomfortable feeling because they aren't yet responsible. You can teach them that quality by increasing the discomfort during the instruction process. We're not suggesting you yell at or be mean to your children. The goal isn't to make them feel uncomfortable with you, but simply to feel uncomfortable with an unfinished assignment. That uncomfortable feeling translates into a sense of obligation to complete the task. Requiring kids to report back puts a definite end to the instruction, freeing children when the task is complete. They feel a bit uncomfortable, knowing that their work will be evaluated and that someone is waiting for them to report back. The uncomfortable feeling is lifted once they report back and their work is checked.

Many parents start instructions well but don't end them effectively. Instead of a feeling of satisfaction of a job well done, the child feels guilty, wondering when Mom is going to find out that he pushed the clothes under the bed or didn't sweep the walk. Parents give their children a gift by requiring that the child report back. If the job wasn't done up to expectations, then the child isn't released until the task is completed. After parents check the work and release the child, they're giving that child the gift of freedom in his or her conscience. The child has completed the task and is now free to go. Unfortunately, many children don't ever receive that gift and instead live with the continual guilt of jobs done incompletely or inadequately.

The story of David in the Old Testament is a fun one for kids, because he was a hero. But being a hero for David didn't start when he killed Goliath. It started much earlier in the small things of life. David, like many children today, took care of the animals. He had sheep duty. He practiced his musical instrument, enabling him to get a job playing for the king as he got a bit older. His father could trust him to do an errand, like take food to the commander of the army. In short, David was responsible early, and God chose this young man to do bigger things for him.

Interestingly enough, David took the place of a king who wasn't responsible. His name was Saul, and he just couldn't seem to obey God. "I am grieved that I have made Saul king," God said, "because he has turned away from me and has not carried out my instructions"

(1 Samuel 15:11). So, the question for your child is, "Would you rather be like David or Saul?" One was faithful in the small things and eventually became a hero. The other had a great job and lost it because he couldn't follow instructions.

The roots of responsibility are taught to children as you teach them to follow directions and report back. It may seem trivial to some, but it provides the foundation for more significant tasks in the future.

45

Much of the benefit of mealtimes is lost when
parents overemphasize manners or diet. Those are
important, but it's also helpful to . . .

Use Mealtimes to Build Relationships

Take a moment and reflect on the conversation around your dinner table. When Rachel thought about it, she realized that the interaction was rather negative, with a continual focus on manners and diet issues. "But what am I supposed to do when they're being silly or are just eating chips and nothing else?"

What children eat is important. A balanced diet is foundational for healthy growth and development. It's no wonder parents are concerned with what their kids eat. Unfortunately, too much focus on diet can contribute to anxiety surrounding eating and food choices. A careful balance is important.

In most of life, eating is a social event. When people gather together, it's usually around food. Why not start now to use mealtimes in your home to build relationships? Allow your meals to become a time to enjoy one another.

Instead of nagging kids about their food choices, it's often best to provide healthy meals and snacks and minimize unhealthy options. If you provide apple slices as a snack for your preschooler, then that's his snack. If your son wants cookies instead, you simply say, "This is our snack today. If you don't want to eat it, then lunch is coming in a bit."

For lunch you might provide a sandwich with some carrot sticks and celery. If your child complains and wants chips instead, you can say, "This is lunch. Eat whatever parts of it you want. We'll be having a snack later."

The natural consequence of not eating is hunger, an excellent motivator. In fact, it's amazing what kids will actually eat when they're hungry. You don't always have to be firm with food choices, but if your child continually chooses chips and cookies instead of eating healthy alternatives, then you may want to take a more firm approach. You don't need a lot of bantering about the subject. Just be firm and matter-of-fact.

Remember that kids eat more or less at different stages of growth. Furthermore, many children have a narrow range of foods that taste good to them. You don't have to cook only what they like. Make a variety of foods, but allow children to opt out of eating what they don't like. Provide healthy snacks between meals, and encourage children to choose from what's available.

Parents who force kids to clean their plates often do their children a disservice. In Western culture we tend to have problems with obesity and food-related anxiety disorders. You don't want to contribute to those problems by being hypervigilant with food. Offer children healthy options, and allow them to choose the quantity.

In many homes, dinnertime is the only time when the family actually gets together. This becomes more pronounced as children get older and schedules become more complicated. It's unfortunate that many parents overemphasize manners or food choices or even use the table talk as a time to go over the offenses of the day to further discipline children.

All these things may be necessary or helpful at times, but be careful not to develop a negative pattern around the table. It's been said that more meals are ruined at the dinner table than at the stove.

Coming to the table whether you're hungry or not is important. When you call your child to come and eat and he says, "I'm not hungry," you may be tempted to allow him to continue to play. But the reality is that mealtimes are a family experience. You want to spend time together and enjoy relationships.

Use mealtimes to share about the day. Talk about things you've learned, and ask the children to talk about their experiences. Children will learn valuable relationship skills, such as listening, asking questions, talking, and telling stories. Gentle reminders about affirming others, not interrupting, or letting someone else speak teach children how to carry on conversations and enjoy others in the process.

Take time to plan the social component of the mealtime. Save stories from the day, jokes or riddles, and think of questions that get your kids talking. Some parents spend a lot of time preparing a meal but don't prepare at all for the dialogue. That's a mistake in many homes where the conversation deteriorates rather quickly and relational opportunities are missed.

Children learn from stories. As you share ways you're growing or incidents that made an impression on your day, children apply them to their own lives. Laughing and being silly can add to a positive sense of family life. When appropriate, share how you have applied God's Word in practical situations by the way you think or act. This helps children see that spirituality isn't just a technique; it's a lifestyle.

Some children make mealtimes a challenge. Hyperactive or overly talkative youngsters can make civilized conversations difficult. Sibling conflict issues spill over into what might otherwise be pleasant conversations. Try to gently move things back on track. Redirect conversation, and distract children by your enthusiasm and energy.

Manners are important in order to relate well to others. Learning how to interrupt graciously, how to pass dishes to one another, and how to eat in a polite way are all important. Teach these lessons over time. Don't overemphasize socially appropriate techniques at every meal or you'll end up with a more militant-looking mealtime than is helpful. Balance teaching of manners with relationship and watch children grow over time.

If a child needs discipline, separate that child from the table and tell him that he's welcome to return when he can act appropriately at the meal. In the meantime, continue to enjoy conversation and relationship with the others who are there.

God promises us a special meal at the end of this world, and Revelation 19:9 says, "Blessed are those who are invited to the wedding supper of the Lamb!" It'll be a feast to celebrate our relationship with Christ. You can be sure that that meal will be a special time of enjoying other relationships too. Surely there will be laughing and telling of stories and simply enjoying the privilege of listening to others. The wedding supper will be all about relationships, and children are going to enjoy it just as their parents do.

Your biblical parenting philosophy must include a good perspective on the kitchen table, because mealtimes now are just practice for that special meal we'll all enjoy. What you are doing today is a reflection of the beauty of the meal that's yet to come.

46

Kids often want privileges but don't yet have the character to manage them effectively. In those moments, they need to learn that . . .

PRIVILEGE AND RESPONSIBILITY GO TOGETHER

MELODY AT AGE THIRTEEN ASKED HER MOM, "HOW old do I have to be before I can babysit?"

Mom was wise enough to respond, "The answer doesn't have to do with age. It has to do with responsibility."

Melody continued, "How will you know when I'm responsible enough?"

"I'll see signs of responsibility at home. I can tell if you are responsible by how you take care of your room and what kind of choices you make when I'm not around."

Parents sometimes give privileges to young people who aren't responsible enough to handle them. Privileges are things like being home alone, having an e-mail account, carrying a cell phone, going to the mall with friends, or being able to stay up late.

Children want privileges and often pressure their parents to give them. A strong biblical parenting philosophy will help you withstand undue pressure and will keep privileges in perspective. Be careful about giving privileges too quickly, and when you do give them to your kids, use them to teach responsibility. "Before I can give you access to the Internet, I have to see that you can take a stand for righteousness, be honest under pressure, and do the right thing when no one is watching." Or, "I'd like to allow you to stay up later, but it means that you have to demonstrate a good attitude during the day. I'm not sure we're there yet."

Parenting is like teaching children how to swim. As children are in deep water, learning to be responsible and mature, parents sometimes start throwing toys to them in the form of privileges. Children are then distracted from the task of learning how to grow up, and parents inadvertently contribute to their kids' failure.

Don't fall into the trap that says you owe your children privileges because all their friends have them. Furthermore, some children believe that the privileges enjoyed in your family are rights. An attitude of entitlement can lead a young person to be ungrateful and demanding.

Jesus told a parable in Matthew 25:14–30 about a landowner who returned to find two servants who had been responsible and one that hadn't been. The landowner said to the responsible servants, "You have been faithful with a few things; I will put you in charge of many things." The landowner was saying something important that we must say to our children day after day in order to teach them about life: privilege and responsibility go together.

When the landowner came to the third servant and saw that he'd not been responsible, he said, "Even the little you have will be taken from you." That should be true in family life as well. Parents must remove privileges from children who aren't responsible.

Another way to say it is this: a young person shouldn't be able to experience the benefits of family life without also abiding by the principles that make it work. One dad said, "I feel uncomfortable taking you to the mall right now because of the way you asked me to leave your room a few minutes ago. First, let's deal with the way you're treating me, and then we can talk about the privilege of having a ride to the mall."

Enforcing the principle that privilege and responsibility go together can be a primary way for parents to discipline their teens. If your son shows a lack of responsibility, don't reward his irresponsibility with privileges, no matter how old he is. Just because a child is fourteen doesn't mean he's mature enough to go to a friend's house without supervision. Don't give privileges based on age; use responsibility as a guide instead.

Responsibility is demonstrated in practical ways. Cleaning up after a snack, taking initiative to help clear the table, being honest in a difficult situation, responding to correction without blaming an offense on someone else, and handling disappointment with a good attitude are all indications of responsibility.

When a parent says no to a privilege, a teen may say, "You don't trust me." And the answer is, "Trust is something you earn by being responsible. Show me that you're responsible with checking in, doing your jobs around the house without being reminded, and taking a stand for righteousness when you're in a difficult situation; then we can talk about you having some of these privileges that you're requesting."

Teens tend to want more freedom. It's best to view that freedom as a privilege and tie it to doing well in several areas. You might say, "Son, I understand you want more freedom. If you're doing well at school by doing your best, at work by being responsible, at home by completing your chores and treating our family with respect, and at church by being involved with the Lord, then I'm more motivated to release you in other areas. Show me responsibility in these key areas of your life and I'll be eager to give you greater privileges."

It's unrealistic to expect that a young child knows how to clean up her bedroom; you teach her and then check up on her. The same is true with teaching responsibility to teens. You can't just assume that a young person knows how to withstand negative peer pressure, for example. It takes work to develop the ability to say no under pressure. If your child hasn't learned how to stand for what's right in that kind of situation (responsibility), be careful about allowing him to go to the mall with his friends (privilege). Children need to learn responsibility, and as a parent, you have the privilege—or shall we say, the responsibility—to teach it.

47

Children need limits. They need correction. Parents must set boundaries and require action, but . . .

FIRMNESS DOESN'T REQUIRE HARSHNESS

"MY KIDS WON'T DO ANYTHING UNLESS I GET ANGRY." This parent is confusing harshness with firmness. They aren't the same thing.

Firmness says that a boundary is secure and won't be crossed without a consequence. Harshness, on the other hand, uses angry words to make children believe parents mean what they say. Ask yourself an important question: What cues do you give your kids that you mean business? Is it anger or is it firmness? If you find yourself being harsh, take time to reevaluate your response. More action and less yelling can go a long way toward bringing about significant change.

For some, this is such a new concept that they have trouble grabbing onto it. One mom said, "The thought of separating firmness from harshness is like listening to a foreign language—it sounds nice but doesn't make any sense." You can use your biblical parenting philosophy to separate them.

How do you make the change to using firmness without harshness? Two things will help you remove harshness from your interaction with your children: dialogue less, and show less emotion.

Don't misunderstand; talking to your kids is good most of the time because it strengthens relationship bonds between parent and child. However, in an attempt to build relationship, some parents spend too much time dialoguing about instructions. They try to defend their words, persuade their children to do what they're told, or logically explain the value of obeying. This is often counterproductive and teaches children how to resist more. Parents then resort to anger to end the discussion, complicating matters further.

"But," one mom said, "I thought talking and showing emotion are signs of a healthy family, leading to closeness in family life." That is true when they're used in the right way. Unfortunately, when added to the instruction process, these two ingredients confuse children and don't give them the clear boundaries they need. These are two good things, just in the wrong place at the wrong time.

Anger works. It quiets children, moves them toward the car when it's time to go, and motivates them to clean their room. But anger and harshness have a downside. They build walls of resistance in children, and over years contribute to distance in relationships.

A good correction routine teaches children that they must change. Their current course of action won't work. It's unacceptable and needs adjusting. Unfortunately, the clear message that the child has a problem and needs to work on it is sometimes missed because of parental anger. A parent's harshness can confuse the learning process. Instead of thinking, *I'm here taking a break because I did something wrong*, the child thinks, *I'm here taking a break because I made Mom mad.*

The child's focus changes from correcting what he or she did wrong to avoiding parental anger. It's important to remember that your anger is helpful for identifying problems but not good for solving them. When you're tempted to respond harshly, be careful to take a moment and think about what you're trying to teach in the situation. It's easy to react with anger when your child is doing the wrong thing, but it's more effective to move into a constructive correction routine.

Firmness requires action, not anger. Having a toolbox of consequences is important to help move children along in life. It's not optional. Some parents use anger as their consequence. These parents need more tools to help their children make lasting changes. In fact, we believe that parents who don't have tools and who don't have a plan use anger to solve problems.

Responding with anger is often a form of revenge, whereas firmness lends itself well to teaching children what to do right and motivating them to do it. Harshness gives a wrong message to kids. For example, Dad yells, "I've had it! I called you five times, and you didn't come, so I'm not taking you to the party!"

The child gets a mixed signal. Is missing the party the consequence for not coming when called, or is it the consequence for making Dad angry? Children who grow up with explosive parents learn to focus more on pleasing people than on living with convictions about right and wrong. Instead of asking, "What is the right thing to do here?" they ask, "How can I maneuver through this situation without making anyone upset?" They may learn to make changes in life, but not because they're determined to do what's right. Rather, they make changes to avoid upsetting people; they become people pleasers or just plain sneaky. Kids then believe that what they did was okay, as long as Mom or Dad didn't find out. As long as no one got angry, then there's no problem.

When you make a mistake and correct in anger, it's important to come back to your child and talk about it afterward. Clarify what was wrong, why the consequence was given, and apologize for your harshness.

The Bible offers this insightful proverb: "The wise woman builds her house, but with her own hands the foolish one tears hers down" (Proverbs 14:1). Obviously the tearing down of a house can be done by a father or a mother. The point is, the inner strength of emotional control not only guides children and builds them up in a positive direction, but it creates greater closeness in relationships.

Proverbs 15:1 is equally perceptive. It says, "A gentle answer turns away wrath, but a harsh word stirs up anger." Keep in mind that harshness gets in the way of the growth you want to see in your children and in your relationships.

48

If kids do the right thing but grumble and complain, then you have a problem. It's not good enough to do what's right if your heart is in the wrong place. That's why you'll want to . . .

DISCIPLINE FOR BAD ATTITUDES

UNFORTUNATELY, SOME PARENTS EXCUSE BAD ATTI-tudes in their children. We've all heard the excuses.

"He'll grow out of it."

"She's so cute."

"At least she's doing what I asked."

"He's tired."

"He's just going through a stage."

"She's better than other kids her age."

"That's the way kids are."

"She's a teenager."

"He's a two-year-old."

"He's a boy."

"She could be a lot worse."

Each of these is an excuse for not disciplining and often represents a missed opportunity to teach or direct a child on a deeper level. Remember, you aren't just trying to help children change on the outside to develop nice, pleasant behavior. You're trying to help your children change their hearts. A good biblical parenting philosophy recognizes that attitude is a window into a child's heart.

Attitudes can be good or bad and are inherently interwoven

192 · THE CHRISTIAN PARENTING HANDBOOK

into everything we do. They often rest just below the surface and are sometimes difficult to read or understand in adults, let alone our children. Billions of advertising dollars are spent each year to create or change attitudes toward certain products or activities. Furthermore, attitudes are highly contagious. As a parent, you know that children can develop a whole outlook on life based on the latest TV show or by spending time with a particular friend. Attitudes affect how we view life and respond to it.

Attitudes become a problem when negative emotions affect behavior and relationships. It's not wrong to feel bad, but when you act out because of those negative feelings, people get hurt. Parents frequently see their kids' bad attitudes when they give their children instructions they'd rather not follow. Those kids may obey, but have a bad attitude in the process.

Often a bad attitude comes from an angry heart. Imagine an onion with various layers. As you peel off one layer, you see another and another until you get to the center of the onion. Anger is like that. The most obvious sign of anger is physical violence. Hitting, slamming, kicking, and biting are all ways that anger is demonstrated.

As children learn to control their physical reactions, they peel off that layer, revealing the next one: hurtful words through sarcasm, teasing, and cynical remarks. These less physical but deadly weapons are another symptom of anger.

Layer after layer of angry responses can be removed until you come to a very significant one: the bad attitude. Children don't want to go to bed, clean up their rooms, leave the computer, or get on their shoes. You're interrupting their lives by giving an instruction or correcting or saying no. Thus, you get anger, revealed through a bad attitude.

One approach for dealing with bad attitudes is to use the concept of honor. It's important to teach children what honor means in very practical terms. One mom defined attitude as "the heart of how you do something." Obedience is revealed in actions. Honor is revealed in the attitude that goes along with those actions.

Many times parents simply focus on the behavioral component of the bad attitude. They say things like, "Stop giving me that dirty look," or "Come back here and walk down the hall without stomping." Keep in mind that to deal with bad attitudes with a heart-based approach, you'll also want to look at two more components: emotions and thinking errors. Both of those ingredients reside in the heart. Children need to process their emotions without demonstrating a bad attitude. Furthermore, many children believe strange things about life. Those beliefs may include, *When my brother is annoying, I have the right to punch him,* or *When I feel uncomfortable, I have the right to make others miserable.* When children believe those kinds of things, it's no wonder they have a bad attitude. Take attitudes apart and work on them using a multifaceted approach. You'll then see more significant and long-lasting adjustments.

By identifying bad attitudes in your children, you'll take the first important step toward change—you'll see the problem. You won't be content to allow a bad attitude, even if the job is getting done. You might say to your son, "Wait a minute. Your attitude here is a problem. I'd like you to sit down for a bit and settle down, and then let's look for a better way to respond. When you're ready to try a different response then we'll continue."

Explain to your children the value of a good attitude and the danger of a negative attitude on the job or in school. A good attitude is important, and your interaction at home is a great place to start working on it.

And always remember that attitude and honor are matters of the heart. In Matthew 15:8, Jesus said of the Pharisees, "These people honor me with their lips, but their hearts are far from me." In other words, the Pharisees focused on behavior instead of their hearts. The same thing is true with children sometimes, and your responsibility is to teach them that their hearts are as important as their actions. Honor is important, but children can't just show honor externally. They must also demonstrate that honor with a positive attitude.

Attitudes are one way that children can reveal that their hearts are in the right place. One mom put a sign up in her kitchen that read, "Attitudes, good or bad, are revealed in three areas: when given an instruction, when corrected, and when given a no answer." She was trying to motivate her kids to recognize the danger arenas and take appropriate action.

Helping children deal with bad attitudes isn't easy. It requires insight from parents into the hearts of their kids. Sometimes you'll want to deal with an attitude on the spot, and other times you may want to address it later. Whatever you do, make sure that you address bad attitudes, or they'll get worse over time. Sometimes parents believe their children will grow out of bad attitudes. Unfortunately, the reality is that if attitudes aren't checked, children often grow into them.

49

Parents sometimes feel overwhelmed by their children's weaknesses. Kids need a lot of help. One of the ways to keep a positive focus is to recognize that the present flaws your children are demonstrating may just be . . .

GOOD CHARACTER QUALITIES MISUSED

ONE MOM TOLD US ABOUT HER SON WHO HAD A genuine sensitivity to others' needs. He was compassionate and cared for others and often felt things deeply. "I remember one time when he was younger, he began to cry when he saw an ambulance speeding down the road because he knew that someone was hurt inside. He's very caring. Unfortunately, sometimes this sensitivity can cause him to become moody or overly emotional, pouting or crying over the least little problem." The positive quality is sensitivity, but it can have a negative side, making a child moody or prone to emotional outbursts.

All children have good character qualities that, when taken to the extreme, have a negative side. One child may be quite organized, but, if not careful, may become inflexible in a less structured situation. It's like the saying, "Your strength can be your greatest weakness."

Another mom saw that her son had the ability to work hard at a task without being distracted. "He focuses intensely, with real determination to succeed." This quality of being persistent can be a real asset, but sometimes it would show itself as stubbornness.

As you look at your children's weaknesses, look for a positive character quality they may be misusing. Then search for ways to balance it with other character qualities. Give praise for the positive quality, and encourage practical ways to bring balance.

Here are a few more good qualities and ways that their misuse may be revealed:

POSITIVE QUALITY	IF MISUSED, THE CHILD CAN BE . . .
Analytical skill	picky, petty, critical
Confidence	prideful, bossy, insensitive, overconfident, determined to always be the leader
Contentedness	unmotivated, apathetic, lazy
Courage	reckless, foolish, incapable of seeing the consequences of actions
Creativity	deceptive, manipulative, mischievous, prone to always have a better way
Determination	hardheaded, stubborn, obstinate, argumentative, badgering
Efficiency	slow to obey, inflexible, demanding, insistent on having things a certain way
Enthusiasm	intense, insensitive, fanatical, extreme, a thrill-seeker
Expressiveness	talkative, wordy, dominating in conversation, a poor listener
Neatness	perfectionist, inflexible, unwilling to share

Identifying positive qualities misused will not only encourage you as a parent, but it will help you develop a strategy for training.

Armando told us this story: "I used to get so irritated by my son's inflexibility. If I didn't give him warning before some kind of change, he'd get upset. But one day I was talking to another father who was frustrated that his son's room was always messy. I mentioned that we don't have that problem in our home. My friend was shocked and told me how blessed I am to have a son who is neat. It was then that I realized that my son's neatness and his inability to be flexible come from the same character strength. He likes order, and when things aren't in order, he has a hard time.

"I still need to work on my son's flexibility, and he needs to be able to go with the flow a little more, but now that I see his character strength, I'm less frustrated as I discipline him. I don't want him to become a slob and give up his orderliness. I just want to bring some other character qualities alongside this one so he can enjoy his strength more fully."

Armando is right, and he'll do well parenting his son in this area. It's sometimes hard to enjoy someone who is very different. The apostle Paul recognized this truth as he looked at God's family, the church. He saw that people all have different gifts and that they have a tendency to minimize the importance of others' qualities. So he gave this advice in Romans 12:6–8: "We have different gifts, according to the grace given us. If a man's gift is prophesying, let him use it in proportion to his faith. If it is serving, let him serve; if it is teaching, let him teach; if it is encouraging, let him encourage; if it is contributing to the needs of others, let him give generously; if it is leadership, let him govern diligently; if it is showing mercy, let him do it cheerfully."

Notice how, when addressing some of these gifts, Paul recommended a character quality to help make the gift stronger. This advice for the church has similar application for the earthly family.

When you recognize a child's strength in an area of character, take time to demonstrate admiration for it. Appreciation tends to focus on what a child does and is important in family life. Admiration focuses on who the child is and goes straight to the heart. When you spend time admiring a child's strengths, you help form beliefs about self. Those beliefs are important because they form the way a child acts and develops.

You might say, "Son, you're an emotional person. I think God gave you an extra scoop of emotions when he designed you. I know you're trying to work on your anger control now, but I just want you to know that I admire your emotional sensitivity. You're the kind of person that livens up a party and who can see a problem developing before others because of the emotional cues. I like that. You do very well, and God is going to use that in your life in some powerful ways, I'm sure."

No character strength can be used as an excuse for a corresponding weakness. We must help our children grow and make improvements in areas that are a challenge, but if we tie those weaknesses to corresponding strengths, we may be able to bring about change more quickly. Each child is unique. Your parenting strategies will be stronger as you take those strengths into account and bring balance to them to make them most effective.

50

Extended family can provide tremendous support for the difficult job of raising children. So, be sure to consider . . .

THE VALUE OF GRANDPARENTS

GRANDPARENTS MEET A SPECIAL NEED IN THE LIVES of their grandchildren. In fact, studies show that kids believe grandparents are very important and value their relationships with them. Furthermore, most grandparents find their role quite rewarding.

Most parents recognize the need to have other adults involved in their children's lives. Kids often listen to other leaders and authorities, and parents inadvertently benefit from the parenting help. Grandparents are an excellent source of strength for grandchildren. Not only is there the emotional bond, but also grandparents have the ability to help grandchildren feel special and embrace family values. (Much credit and applause should go to those grandparents who are raising their grandchildren today. Just at a time of life when they thought their parenting days were over, they begin again to meet parenting challenges with younger kids.)

The strength of the relationship between grandparents and their grandchildren comes in part because of the one-generation step between them. Grandparents can love the kids, hear the reports, give some wisdom and love, but aren't usually involved in the day-to-day work of parenting. This one factor contributes to significant relational benefits for a family. Grandparents can often contribute opinions about ways to handle the tensions of family life, or give the

199

kids an opportunity to tell their stories, both good and bad, to a loving, listening ear.

Grandparents are often supportive during stressful times in a family's life. Not only can they offer babysitting and respite care for parents who want to enjoy some time alone, but they can be a sturdy support during times of crisis, such as the loss of a loved one or a divorce or separation.

If relationships between you and your parents or in-laws are strained, the arrival of a new child can be just the bridge necessary to begin healing between you and them. In fact, many moms and dads have learned to appreciate the struggles of their own parents as new parenting problems reveal that raising kids isn't as easy as it looks.

At times you may be frustrated with your parents and the way they interact with your kids. Overindulgence is one of the most frequent complaints parents have about the grandparent/grandchild interaction. You may need to set some limits on gifts, or teach your child how to handle possessions in those situations, but don't miss the great benefit that's developing. Children can learn gratefulness and develop nonmaterialistic ways of building relationship. Of course, grandparents love the greeting cards, video messages, and specially baked treats much more than monetary gifts anyway.

Grandparents are people. That means they have their own set of strengths and weaknesses. Don't spend a lot of time wishing your parents or in-laws were different. Look for ways to take advantage of the good and minimize the bad. This can only help your kids.

When possible, look to your parents and in-laws for strength, information, and wisdom. They can be a stress reliever for frustrated children, arbitrators in a disagreement, and avid supporters to provide encouragement even during times of failure. Grandparents can be watchdogs, identifying weaknesses in parents and kids, as well as impending dangers. They can be family historians and offer stories that can teach important lessons to children.

Grandparents often like to joke and kid, bring surprises, and take kids on special trips. Many children look to grandparents to be a safe place they can go to for advice. Grandparents can give perspective to their grandkids about growing up, and what maturity looks like. In short, grandparents become a stabilizing force within a family.

Kids often don't understand the complexity of a grandparent's weaknesses, and you don't have to elaborate on them. Just look for ways to use grandparents to reinforce the things you're already doing in your kids. It's amazing how powerful grandparents' words, gifts, and encouragement can be. Those things can send a message that says to a child, "You're part of something bigger here. You're part of a family, and you're carrying on a legacy as you grow up and become the person God wants you to be."

Genesis 48:1–22 tells a beautiful story of Joseph taking his two sons to their grandfather for a blessing. In verse 9 Grandpa said, "Bring them to me so I may bless them." As the story unfolds, Grandpa's blessing meant a lot to those boys, and God used it in their future as well. If your parents are believers, ask them regularly to pray for your kids and with your kids. Imparting a spiritual blessing on them passes on a heritage that comes not from an earthly lineage but from a heavenly one.

Children benefit greatly from grandparents, and you can do a lot to encourage your kids to spend time with them. They're often the hidden blessing in a family. Take the time to nurture those relationships. Your kids will be better for it.

Conclusion

Every once in a while, after hearing us teach a parenting seminar, a distressed parent will come up and say, "I wish I'd known this information before. Is it too late? I think I've ruined my kids." One parent recently asked that question, and I (Scott) said, "How old are your children?"

She replied, "Six and seven."

I smiled and gently explained that it's never too late.

Here's a mom of relatively young children, wondering if she missed out. I helped her realize that it's never too late to help children grow up. In fact, many parents are still trying to influence their adult children toward maturity and wisdom.

As you drive down a highway, you can see that there are lines in the road to keep you on track. Those lines are helpful because they allow you to avoid accidents and keep moving in the right direction. Similarly, a biblical philosophy of parenting helps you stay focused and encouraged as you travel the road of parenting. This is especially helpful on hard days, but even good days can cause the best parents to move a bit off their intended path. Making small adjustments and continually checking the map to be sure you're going in the right direction are important.

Hopefully you took our advice in the introduction of this book and began creating a TO DO list and a THINK list as you read through the chapters. Those ideas will help give you perspective. As you implement your ideas, you'll likely encounter resistance. Just remember that the Christian life is a daily experience, and change takes place over time. Your job isn't to bring instant change in your family. Rather, you want to trust God every day for opportunities to bring about the change he desires. God gives his grace to parents and children along the way. Sometimes you just have to stand under the spigot of God's grace for a while to get recharged and empowered to move forward.

Consider your family as if they were in therapy. We believe that you, the parent, are the best therapist for your child, if you have a good plan. Hopefully, over the course of this book, you've been able to formulate a clearer idea of what that plan looks like for you. Pray now that God will help you fine-tune the plan and begin to put it into practice. Work your plan over time, and trust that God will use it to bring about the wholeness you long for in yourself and your kids.

Therapy involves work. If you get physical therapy for your shoulder, it means that the normal activity you do is not enough. Likely that same concept will apply to your family. You'll not just change the way you do things, but you'll have to practice the new responses. They may not feel comfortable or productive at the time, but, knowing that you're doing the right thing and are headed in the right direction, do them anyway.

But don't rest your hope in a person, or a book, or even a parenting philosophy. Your hope needs to be in God himself. Isaiah 40:31 says, "Those who hope in the LORD will renew their strength. They will soar on wings like eagles; they will run and not grow weary, they will walk and not be faint." It's your hope in the Lord that will continue to drive you forward and empower you to do the work of parenting when the challenges come. Stay focused and enjoy the ride, not just the destination, as you continue to grow in your own relationship with Jesus and your relationships in your family.

Sometimes well-meaning teachers, in order to motivate you to spend positive time with your children when they're young, say,

"You have to love and affirm your kids early in life because their self-concept is developed by the time they're five years old." But what if your child is six? Does that mean it's too late? Others say, "You have to work hard to teach convictions to your children early because their worldview is developed by the time they're twelve." That makes sense, but what if your child is thirteen? Have you totally missed out?

Although these teachers have good intentions, they're relying on a humanistic model of child development. On the other hand, a biblical parenting philosophy recognizes that God changes people at any age. He changes people at five and six, at twelve and thirteen. He even changes people at thirty-five, forty-five, and even older. God can change each one of us no matter how old we are.

And where does God do this work? He does it in the heart. When you ask Jesus to come into your life, he sets up shop and throws out the old value system and builds a whole new one.

One of the many benefits of a heart-based approach to parenting is that you can start it at any age. By appealing to the heart, you're working on the child's operating system, and major changes can take place as parents and children work on issues.

God changed the apostle Paul from someone who fought and killed Christians to a man who lovingly cared for them and won many converts to the faith. Don't ever give up on your kids. They need you to believe in them and believe that God will continue the work he's started.

Even if you've made significant mistakes in the past, don't give up or berate yourself. Do the best job of parenting you can now. Ask God to continue to grow you and help you become the parent that he wants you to be. God delights in turning the hearts of the parents to their kids and the hearts of the kids to their parents. In fact, according to Malachi 4:6, that's one of the signs of the end times: "He will turn the hearts of the fathers to their children, and the hearts of the children to their fathers."

God created the family to be a laboratory for growth for both parents and children. In fact, many parents, it seems, learn more from their kids than the other way around. There's nothing like having kids to teach patience, anger management, self-control, and perseverance. It's a good thing you don't have to be a parenting expert to raise children!

One of the greatest qualities parents need is a willingness to be teachable. If you're always learning and growing, you'll be able to flex with your child's challenges, adapt to the developmental stages, and make the necessary parenting shifts to keep up with your kids.

One of the reasons God gave imperfect parents to kids is so we would all long for the perfect Parent. Isn't it interesting that God has chosen the picture of the family to describe the kind of relationship he wants to have with us? He wants to become our heavenly Father. In fact, that's the most important element in a biblical parenting philosophy that anyone could embrace.

If you haven't yet trusted Jesus Christ as your personal Savior, then please consider making that decision today. You want to get to know God as Father, not as a distant God, out there beyond reach. God wants to walk through the challenges of your life with you every day. It all starts by trusting Jesus as your Lord and Savior.

As we said before, parenting is the toughest job in the world. We need all the help we can get. Getting to know God as heavenly Father provides all kinds of spiritual resources needed for parenting. When you feel discouraged because of how far you or your children need to go, remember the encouraging words that Paul gave to the Corinthians: "He will keep you strong to the end, so that you will be blameless on the day of our Lord Jesus Christ" (1 Corinthians 1:8).

It's never too late to influence your children. Keep praying, and enjoy the hope God gives to us all. He's in the business of changing people.

INDEX

Hebrews
  4:12, 7
  12:1, 58
  12:11, 100
James
  1:5, 142
  1:19, 109
  1:20, 81, 108
  1:22–25, 13
  5:16, 174
1 Peter
  2:13–14, 139
  4:8, 89
2 Peter 3:18, 19
1 John 1:9, 174
Revelation
  3:20, 25
  19:9, 183

A
Abraham, 118
accountability, 177
action point, 116–119
Adam and Eve, 130–131
admiration, 197
admitting wrong, 129
affirming godly character, 17
age
  for change, 204
  and privileges, 186
analytical skill, misuse risks, 196

anger
  alternatives, 80
  of child, 27, 144–148
  communicating action
    point without, 117
  as motivation, 92, 117
  of parent, 65, 188–189
  preventing, 107–110
  as response to mistake, 79
  vs. sorrow, in discipline
    process, 7
  and spanking, 133
anger management plan, 144,
  146–147
anxiety disorders, 181
appreciation, 197
arguments, 68–71
attentiveness, 16
attitude, 151
  discipline for bad,
    191–194
  good vs. negative, 193
authoritarian approach, 69
authority
  responsiveness to, 36, 118,
    139
  supporting others working
    with children, 136–139
awareness, of emotional state,
  112–113

About the Authors

Dr. Scott Turansky and Joanne Miller, RN, BSN are the founders of the National Center for Biblical Parenting. Their heart-based approach to parenting is revolutionizing families. Instead of relying on simple behavior modification, they provide best practice tools that have greater effectiveness for lasting change. They are the authors and editors of numerous books, parent training curricula, and children's programs designed to strengthen families. Turansky and Miller are also the founders of Biblical Parenting University, providing parents with easy access to parent training through online courses. They work with the 4/14 Window Movement to help parents around the world pass the faith on to their kids and mobilize churches to equip them.

biblicalparenting.info
biblicalparentinguniversity.com
TakeTheFamilyChallenge.com
Email: parent@biblicalparenting.org

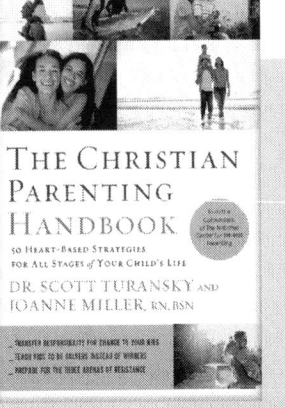

Free
E-mail Parenting
Tips

Receive guidance and inspiration a couple of times a week in your inbox. Free Parenting Tips give practical suggestions to help you relate better to your kids and help your kids change their hearts, not just their behavior.

The National Center for Biblical Parenting is here to help you. Visit biblicalparenting.info and sign up today for Free E-mail Parenting Tips, available in English and Spanish. While you're there, discover other great resources for parents.

76 Hopatcong Drive, Lawrenceville, NJ 08648-4136
Phone: (609) 771-8002
E-mail: parent@biblicalparenting.org
Web: biblicalparenting.info

Printed in Great Britain
by Amazon